Praise for Chantal Morales McKinney and *Following Jesus Beyond Church Walls*

"Chantal McKinney is a brave and necessary truth-teller, unafraid to name harm and yet unwilling to surrender hope. Her voice is helping chart a new way forward—one rooted in integrity, resilience, and a fierce commitment to the liberating way of Jesus."
—Rev. Dr. Amy Butler, pastor of Community Church of Honolulu, founder of Invested Faith, and the first woman to lead the historic Riverside Church in New York City

"*Following Jesus Beyond Church Walls* is a courageous and tender invitation to reclaim faith after spiritual harm. Chantal McKinney names what too many women have endured in silence and guides readers toward a love-centered, expansive Christianity rooted not in institutions, but in Christ. This book is for anyone who has been wounded by church but still longs for Jesus."
—Dr. Andrew J. Bauman, author of *Safe Church: How to Guard Against Sexism & Abuse in Christian Communities*

"In *Following Jesus Beyond Church Walls*, Chantal McKinney courageously shares her own story of fracture and betrayal at the hands of the church—naming not only the harm she endured, but how that harm was multiplied by the institution's broken response. Through her healing, Chantal offers hard-won spiritual wisdom and casts a mystical, magnetic vision of a church beyond its walls, inspiring us by reminding us that 'there is nowhere God is not.' This book belongs in the hands of anyone seeking a faith that tells the truth and still dares to hope."
—The Rev. Elle Dowd, author of *Baptized in Tear Gas: From White Moderate to Abolitionist*

"*Following Jesus Beyond Church Walls* feels like sitting across from someone who has walked through fire and still believes in love. Chantal Morales McKinney offers a fully brave and gentle invitation to anyone who has felt their faith outgrowing the container it was first poured into. She writes with an expansive honesty, carrying a love for Christ that refuses to shrink or harden. This book is a reminder that when our faith begins to stretch, it may feel like we are rebelling. We aren't. We are just growing. We are just being called to follow Jesus into mystery with courage."
— John Roedel, comic, author of *Hey God. Hey John.*

"With courageous honesty, Chantal Morales McKinney offers a candid reckoning with harm she endured within the church and the failures that allowed it to persist. As she grieves alongside the countless women whose suffering has gone unheard and unchecked, she refuses to let the story end in despair. Instead, she issues a hope-filled call to action: change is possible. It begins within our own hearts and extends outward, reshaping the institutional church and transforming communities of faith into places of justice, safety, and healing."
—David Hayward (NakedPastor), author of *Questions Are The Answer*

"This book is for deconstructing Christians, exvangelicals, spiritual seekers, and anyone searching for God beyond church walls. A modern-day Christian mystic and Episcopal priest, Chantal Morales McKinney explores an expansive faith in Christ that makes room for others while calling the church toward justice, reform, and healing. This book opens readers to spiral fractals, the divine feminine, and seeing, praying, and living with Christ-eyes—loving, spiritual eyes. Chantal inspires us to form communities that resonate and spiral outward with that all-loving, inclusive divine vision."
—Eady Jay (EDJ), podcaster and author of *Reconstructing Sexual Ethics*

"*Following Jesus Beyond Church Walls* is an honest, faith-filled, engaging description of Chantal McKinney's journey as an ordained priest through the trauma of sexual abuse, and the way in which it brought her to the realization of a crisis currently plaguing the institutional Church. She describes what the Church needs to do in order to heal and live its mission effectively, and she lays out a clear vision of what that future Church can be. *Following Jesus Beyond Church Walls* offers a vision of what a renewed Church looks like, and a pathway by which it can be realized. There is something here for every committed seeker of God."

—Sister Carolyn McWatters, RSM

FOLLOWING JESUS BEYOND CHURCH WALLS

FOLLOWING JESUS BEYOND CHURCH WALLS

A Catalyst for Your Spiritual Growth

CHANTAL MORALES MCKINNEY

Copyright © 2026 Chantal McKinney

All rights reserved.

No part of this book may be reproduced or transmitted in any form or by any means, electronic or mechanical, including photocopying, recording, or by any information storage and retrieval system, without prior written permission of the author, except for brief quotations used in reviews.

For permission requests, contact: chantalmckinney.com/contact

Disclaimer: This book contains memoir-based reflections and theological commentary drawn from my personal experiences, observations, and interpretations. This is the true story of my lived experience, based on my own memories and interpretations of events. I understand memories can be subjective and degraded by time and trauma. Nevertheless, efforts have been made to ensure accuracy. I have also included stories of another victim, which was recounted to me. This story has been published with permission from that victim for informational purposes. I have changed details to protect the privacy of those involved. While I believe the story comes from a reliable and credible source, I am not responsible for any inaccuracies in that account. This work addresses experiences of harm within religious and church contexts and may include difficult or sensitive material. The content is offered for purposes of storytelling, reflection, education, and dialogue. It is not intended as a substitute for professional counseling, pastoral care, medical treatment, legal advice, or mental health services. Readers are encouraged to seek appropriate professional support as needed. The theological views expressed are those of the author and do not necessarily represent the beliefs or positions of any church, denomination, organization, or publisher.

Scripture quotations are taken from the New Revised Standard Version Updated Edition. Copyright © 2021 National Council of Churches of Christ in the United States of America. Used by permission. All rights reserved worldwide.

First Edition

Published by Contemporary Mystics Publishing
Winston-Salem, North Carolina
www.contemparymysticspublishing.com

Library of Congress Control Number: 2026901804

Cover image used under license from Shutterstock.com

ISBN: 978-1-971589-00-8 (paperback)
ISBN: 978-1-971589-01-5 (e-book)

Printed in the United States of America

*For Bryson, Moses, Isaac, and Maria Bella:
I love you to the end of the multiverse and back.*

*For all who long for, seek, imagine, cultivate, and co-create
our next stage of being the body of Christ.
For anyone who needed to leave their church.*

For women of all faiths.

Table of Contents

INTRODUCTION: The Spiral of Spiritual Growth and Expansion 1

PART ONE: ROOT
Past to Present

1. The Shattering 11
2. When You Stand Up for Justice,
   the World Will Rise to Meet You 32
3. Daring to Look at the Shadow Side of Church
   and Patriarchy with Christ Eyes 42
4. Burying the Seeds of Lament /
   I Will Not Walk Away from Jesus 54

PART TWO: THRIVE
A New Understanding—The Eternal Present

5. Christ Consciousness:
   Resurrection of a New Understanding 72
6. Listening for God's Rhema
   (God's Word to You) 95
7. A New Era of Divine Feminine Rising:
   The Return of the Divine Mother 110
8. Co-creating Your Life and Our World 141

PART THREE: SOAR
An Expansive Christianity—The Future Is Now

9. A Vision of Future Church 169
10. Awaken and Rise, Guardians of the Faith! 196
11. Meeting the Cosmic Mother Within 222

EPILOGUE: Return to the River 229
AFTERWORD:
An Invitation for the Spiral Fractal to Continue through You 232
APPENDIX:
Quotes from Religions and Faiths of the World 234

Introduction

These days it feels like the entire world is experiencing labor pains. Upheaval and change are in the air. It seems like old constructs are breaking open while we are in the painful process of birthing new ways of being. Environmentalists, Indigenous prophets, political analysts, astrologers, historians, poets, friends, and neighbors are, in their own way, acknowledging these tumultuous times. Cycles of change are upon us. We are witnessing the breaking open of entire industries and systems, which can provoke feelings of unease, chaos, and insecurity, as well as hope for a better way. It seems like everywhere we turn, corruption shouts and yells, drawing attention to itself when it is revealed, while many who live and work quietly with honesty and integrity go unseen. We hope that revelations of corruption and excess greed that disturb our peace eventually lead to reform, advancement, and a nobler way. We wonder what we can do to support that happening when we are just a small part of these massive systems. Revelations pertaining to church, spirituality, and God can also feel uneasy as our traditional understanding is shaken and challenged. Yet these necessary labor pains lead to new life and spiritual growth, ultimately drawing us closer to God.

If life has taught me anything, it's that we are meant to be constantly evolving and expanding. Our constructs, perceptions, insights, and our faith are meant to grow and evolve. I am of the firm belief that an evolving faith and a growing concept of God undergirds and shapes the advancements made in other areas of life because God is Love and we are interconnected through this Love. My concept of love and the meaning of life has evolved and expanded since I was a child. How we look back on our life, our concept of God, and our view of others is meant to develop and expand. This mirrors the patterning found throughout all of nature. The book you are reading is intended to accompany and support your continual spiritual growth and expansion, as that is an inherent pattern of all of life. This book will show you how spiritual expansion can mirror the sacred geometry of a spiral fractal.

A fractal is a repeating pattern that continues outward by its very nature. Fractals in general, and spiral fractals in particular, are found throughout our body, in nature, and the cosmos. Spiral fractal examples include galaxies, hurricanes, snail and nautilus shells, flower petals, and curly hair. The neurons in our brains, our lungs, the structure of our veins, plants, river systems, clouds, crystals, and geographic terrains are also examples of spiral fractals as a pattern of creation. Additionally, Jesus prays in a spiral fractal in the Gospel of John, Chapter 17. He begins by praying for himself, then the community, and finally, the world. Like Jesus' prayer, this book follows the divine patterning of a spiral fractal and invites the reader on the same journey.

The unfolding of this book includes three parts along with reflection questions after each chapter to support you in your ongoing journey towards a more expansive understanding of the Divine. The spiral fractal of spiritual expansion outward continues repeating. Imagine a seashell that spirals outward, getting bigger and more expansive as it curves around each turn.

Our souls, too, have an innate desire to expand like a spiral fractal, something that is not usually supported by American Christian culture, with its consumeristic focus that often keeps the religious experience of churchgoers inside a church building and prioritized over the physical needs of those in poverty in the community. In contrast, this book unfolds like a flower, starting with a close look at how we view our selves and God and then opening to how we can awaken consciousness and impact ourselves and the world by understanding divinity within. The book will support and guide you as you self-reflect through each chapter, accompanying you as you shift and awaken.

This book is intended to support anyone wanting to expand spiritually, no matter their religion of origin or where they find themselves now on their spiritual journey. That being said, I want to be transparent that I fully embrace spiritual expansion while still being a follower of Jesus. Many Christians have not experienced expansiveness in the form of Christianity they were or are a part of. In the last twenty-five years, forty million people have left Christianity because they could no longer find a home in their church. For those open to it, I hope the Scripture verses and insights included will open the reader up to the possibility that there are many ways to follow Jesus. To be clear, this book has not been written with the hopes that you end up in one particular denomination or that churches' membership numbers increase. My intention is to support your spiritual journey, rooted in love, wherever that takes you.

In taking the shape of a spiral fractal, the book begins with the relationship between the individual and the organized religion that is the container that holds the concept of God they were raised with. We explore the root of who we are, our connection to God, and the often-hidden sides of ourselves and our church. As the book expands outward, the reader travels alongside me as I explore encountering God after the shattering of the container I was raised with.

My understanding of what I am writing about also evolves, leading to various descriptions and names for concepts. For example, I use many names to describe God: God, Spirit (a way to describe God I heard often when growing up, usually from my Brazilian godparents, and which is also common in Indigenous North American cultures), Divine Love, Love, Energy of Divine Love, Divine Mother, Divine Father, She, He, Goddess. I invite you to explore what feels right for you and allow yourself to try on other names, particularly if it expands your understanding of our one God.

Introduction

In Part One, I begin with my own dark night of the soul. I describe how my understanding of church shattered after experiencing clear sexual harassment from the senior priest at a church where I was serving as an associate priest. Consider this to be your invitation to take care of yourself while reading if you too have been harmed. My understanding of the harm I endured also evolved as time passed. My bishop refused to name what I endured as sexual harassment, although it was obviously at least that. At that point in the United States, before the Me Too movement, sexual harassment was not often talked about or named. Yet my health care providers and attorney said that what I experienced could be considered not only harassment, but sexual assault, as I experienced physical contact with the intent to harm. My various words for what I endured reflect my evolving understanding. I intentionally do not share an excess of details about what I endured. I do not intend for my story to be salacious in any way, but I do intend to point out the deceit and harm, and my experience of fear, trauma, and lack of transparency. I intentionally do not reveal the names of the church leaders involved, not to protect them, but to point to the fact that this is a systemic problem in the church. My experience of sexual harassment in the church is just one story among those of many other women who have experienced misogyny and harm.

Similarly, my concept of church continues to evolve. I use a lowercase "c" for church to emphasize inclusion over hierarchy, and I seek to expand our concept of church to Jesus' understanding that "when two or three are gathered, I am with them." Church-as-business, church-as-empire, and other terms allow me to differentiate what I experienced from a truer expression of a faith community rooted in Christ. I know that the term "church" carries with it negative connotations for many people who have experienced judgement, hate, and harm within church. I seek to reclaim the word, liberating it from being understood only as a faith community with a building and paid clergy.

After reading my story, some may wonder why I chose to share it. It was the most shameful, terrifying, awful, humiliating time of my life.

To be completely honest, I initially didn't want to include that part in the book. Why would I want to describe it, let alone share it publicly? Why on earth would I want to air my dirty laundry for anyone to see and criticize me about?

I'm not a fool. I know that my story will anger people. I know that I will be judged again. I know that I will face gaslighting and be called names. But I also know the spirit of Jesus Christ. I know that Christ moves through those cracks in our lives. I know that in my own vulnerability, weakness, and surrender, Christ is made strong. After the dark night of my soul, I experienced healing and rising again. I experienced renewal and an uncommon closeness with God. If sharing this part of my life aids other women and other people, then it will be worth it. If sharing this horrendous part of my story allows you to see how far God has brought me in my healing and my thriving, knowing that the same is possible for you and others, it will be worth it.

This book is born from the journey I took to heal my life. More than healing even, this is about going from being wounded to flourishing. Healing implies that once the wound is healed, one goes on as they once were, perhaps with a little scar. But that's not what happened to me. I went from walking to crawling. I was, literally, in a fetal position, my heart in searing pain at my lowest. And on my knees quite a bit. But my abuelita was right when she taught me a powerful prayer that doesn't change outside circumstances but changes the way I perceive the situation and people around me. Over time I went from walking to flying to soaring like an eagle, with ease and flow. The shattering open and labor pains didn't last forever.

Part Two of the book is Thrive, when we develop the ability to sense, perceive, and communicate with the all-encompassing Divine Love of God, removed from the confines and boxes of denominational identities and church walls. Part Three is Soar, when we do this together, in community.

As we explore these ideas together, there may be times that you wonder how to do something that is suggested—how to honor the sabbath, for example. Know that I am writing a second book that is a guidebook to support readers' practical next steps.

I pray that you feel the same energy of possibility, hope, and renewal I experience as you read this book: You who are in need of healing. You who have experienced injustice. You who see the breaking open of entire industries everywhere you turn, including the messaging about God that you were raised with. You who have been on your knees in a time of sorrow and need help getting up again. You who have managed to get up again but now want to flourish and soar instead of going back to the way things have always been. You who have longed for a mystical experience of God that eludes you in church. You who seek, search, and yearn for an encounter that will give you hope and renewal. This book is for you. With God, all things are possible. With love, all things are possible. I pray this book may support your journey to seek, to uncover, to heal, to thrive, to soar, and to expand beyond what you thought was possible.

This book is for anyone who is looking for support beyond what a typical church might offer. To be clear, I do not advocate leaving one's church if you are supported and nourished there. Nor do I advocate feeling guilty if you prefer not to go to church as we currently define it.

Over time, the spiritual expansion I underwent resulted in a deep re-alignment and connection with both Creator and creation. I have prayed to see things the way Christ sees them, and I have been shown what that means for my life. Now the time has come to share what I have experienced and learned with you, to help guide you to discover what an expansive faith looks like for you. How do you enter into the expanse of Divine Love? How can you nurture your own spiritual growth, rooted in Love? What brings your spirit to a sense of joy and union with others and with Love? This book includes the wisdom of my journey to draw closer to God as I seek spiritual growth, but what is God saying to *you* in the quiet of your heart? What is breaking open in the realm of Christianity, and what new expressions of faith, spirituality, and belonging are being born? This book is not meant to be prescriptive. Rather, it seeks to support you in coming closer to listening to the wisdom revealed in you and through you.

These are some of the questions this book will help you answer. Most importantly, I hope my words show you a truth that Jesus knew to be true: our divinity is within us, it exists all throughout the Earth, and knowing how to observe and communicate with the divine-in-all-things changes absolutely everything.

PART ONE: ROOT

Past to Present

1

The Shattering

When the lens through which we were taught to view the world begins to crack, and then shatters and breaks open, it is impossible at first to see through our own devastation. But gradually a new way of seeing and understanding, more beautiful than before, can emerge. I remember the exact moment that my faith in church shattered, like a thousand glass pieces, each one piercing my wounded heart. My heart was already in shock, damaged, and in a state of trauma after enduring several weeks of sexual harassment and threats from the rector (senior priest) at the Episcopal church where I was serving as an associate rector, but the death blow was actually what happened after the harassment.

I received a call from my bishop and his words literally brought me to my knees on my bedroom floor, as though I had been punched in the gut. I was paralyzed by sorrow and fear of the news of what would soon come. Paralyzed, too, by a broken heart. Down the hall, I heard faint squeals of delight from my two boys, ages two and four, who were playing with their Legos. It was almost time for me to make dinner, but like a wounded animal, I couldn't move. My tears soaked the carpet; my stomach tied itself in knots. I was sure I would never recover from this shocking turn of events. The aftermath of this phone call created a scar so profound that it is etched into my soul, to be carried with me for an eternity. This wasn't supposed to happen to me. Where was God? Why was I being abandoned by God and the church? Suddenly, my faith in the church that had sustained me for years was nowhere to be found.

The Universal Mystic

When I was a little girl, I would sit on the back porch swing facing the woods in our North Carolina home, with the stream gurgling a short distance away, the birds singing all around me, and the melodic hum of insects carrying through the humid air of summer in the South. The swing creaked as I swayed back and forth and chatted to the angels and fairies in Mother Nature. The forest was magical to me. Life was magical, actually. I was the oldest sibling with big hazel eyes, a cowlick in her bangs and long brown hair in a ponytail. I had a curly-haired brother two years younger than me whose brown eyes shined with curiosity and intelligence. He loved the animals of the forest, especially frogs. My little sister was feisty and confident, with a mischievous glint in her hazel eyes and long dark brown hair. With only five years in between us, we were thick as thieves. We lived on nine acres, which included fields, a stream with large rocks perfect for children to sit on or hop across the water, and our enchanting forest. Even though my parents had divorced, my dad and stepmom lived only ten minutes away and we saw them all the time. I was raised by loving parents and couldn't have asked for a more wholesome upbringing. We were active in church, in after-school activities, and were well cared for. We grilled out, explored deep into the woods, played basketball in the back yard, and walked to Krispy Kreme for fresh donuts on the weekends after dinner. I collected unicorn stickers, went to baseball games, rode my bike with my siblings, and had a fairly ideal childhood. It was my faith that was uncommon. I believed in Jesus, of course. But I also believed farther out, to the mystical realms of gnomes and unicorns, angels, fairies, and spirit guides. I would talk and sing and commune with them with the purity of a child whose faith was as wide as the sky. I knew they could hear me. I would praise the beauty and wonder of the earth. I sang to the spirits who were in and amidst the trees, the animals, and the plants. Even at an early age, I could feel the interconnectedness and sacredness of nature. I would delight in simple games in the creek with my brother and sister. I gathered eggs from our chickens and helped my dad milk our goats. I ate strawberries fresh from our garden. The world was full of magic, and I felt it most strongly in the forest. Without even knowing it, I was in perfect alignment with creation. A key part of that feeling of perfect alignment was the ongoing dialogue taking place between my heart and Jesus'.

My connection to God was alive and palpable to me. I had a good experience growing up in our Episcopal church. Sunday school and acolyting were taught by loving adults who genuinely cared for children. I loved the outreach we did in our youth group, the youth group ministers, my friends, and the rector in our church. And yet, as good as that was, it was just one part of my faith. My mom, who was Mexican American, lived in Brazil when she served in the Peace Corps and met the family that would become our godparents. They were Christians who practiced Spiritism, a Brazilian practice that involves communicating with spirits. My mom taught me how to meditate as a child. I learned Reiki (a Japanese from of energy healing using the hands) from a Reiki master when I was 12 and regularly attended meditation conferences and trainings with my mom. I loved being in the presence of God in silent meditation. My mom taught us how to cultivate our intuition. We practiced—making little games of it. I learned how to wake up at a precise time without an alarm clock—down to the minute. Sometimes, when we didn't go to church, we would have "church at home," and my mom would teach us simple spiritual principles. We learned how to welcome silence. We learned how to listen to God and not just pray words. We learned about shining our Christ light and sending light to others. We learned from our parents about the importance of serving others who society judged. We believed

The Shattering

in spirit guides and angels that were there for us when we called upon them, in addition to Jesus and the Virgen de Guadalupe,[1] whose image, along with the cross, was in almost every room of our home. My faith was strong and pure, a bright light that shone in my heart. My faith poured out into a belief that God's love was all around me, in singing birds and the gurgling stream. My faith was magical.

I also had the heart of a seeker. Although I was content at church, I longed to encounter God in many different expressions—my soul was hungry for this! In my teen years, some friends and I became enchanted with Hare Krishna. I never saw my curiosity and longing to experience other faiths as a threat to my Christian faith. I knew we honored the same God, in different ways. I liked the discipline of their prayers and chants, the vegetarianism, and the gorgeous colors, flavors, and music, and dancing as a form of worship. I loved that they adored God, like me. Many of them loved and revered Jesus very much, noting the similarity between Krishna and Christ. There was a temple not too far from my home that offered a Sunday feast, prayers, and singing. I eventually became a practitioner of Bhakti Yoga, which is a form of loving devotion to God. The profound feeling of joy I felt in my heart when singing and dancing in the temple awakened my heart in a way that Episcopal worship, which was more traditional with less emotion, did not. My heart leaped at the chance to be in adoration of God with others who were Hare Krishna. I read the Bhagavad Gita several times, as well as other Upanishadic Scriptures. In college I woke before dawn to spend more than an hour each day chanting the Maha Mantra in Sanskrit. Chanting this mantra could elevate me to the same spiritual heights that humans have chased after for thousands of years through the use of herbs and drugs. I thrived with this discipline and devotion. Over time, though, I began to question certain rules. I was happy to be vegetarian, but why did I have to forgo garlic, onion, eggs, and mushrooms? Why was I supposed to forgo caffeine? I was taught that these foods altered the brain and could therefore alter our spirit of devotion. Eggs weren't allowed because they weren't from the cow, who was sacred in India. I also didn't like the comments about my appearance. One male leader would say that I was a gift from Krishna because my beauty would help to attract others to Hare Krishna. He meant it as a compliment, but I felt belittled because my worth was reduced to my looks without consideration for my heart, my faith, or my devotion to God.

In college, I was farther away from the temples, and while I remained active for a while, I bristled at the excessive rules. My seeker heart also wanted to explore other ways of encountering God. One morning, I looked around my apartment at the images of Krishna and Radha, the feminine essence of God and also Krishna's partner. I looked at the images of Jesus and Mary, who were always with me. And then I took a pan out and placed it on the stove. I sauteed onions and garlic in butter and then added mushrooms. Finally, I added eggs and made the most delicious omelet. I savored each bite of the forbidden. When my plate was clean, I looked at the many expressions of the Divine on the walls in my apartment and I knew that I didn't love God any less. I made a decision that I would no longer be controlled by those rules.

I continued to seek after the Divine throughout college. I wanted desperately to attain a spiritual union with the Divine like J. Krishnamurti. I read his books. I read the Tao Te Ching, Buddhist Scriptures, the Koran, Parmahansa Yogananda's autobiography, and my well-worn Bhagavad Gita. I worshipped in temples, in synagogues, with the Bahai, and with Unitarian Universalists. I sat in silence with Buddhists and Quakers. By my last year in college, I had the nagging feeling that it was time to go deeper in Christianity, so I took an Intro to New Testament course. In my NT course, we were supposed to read a gospel all the way through, like a book. This was quite different than hearing short Bible passages here and there on Sunday mornings as I did growing up. I'll never forget sitting in my most comfortable chair, with tea next to me, and reading the Gospel of Luke like a novel. Never in my life have I experienced falling in love by reading pages in a book, but I fell head over heels in love with Jesus. I loved everything about him. I loved his values. I loved his teachings. I loved his subversiveness. I loved the way he used ragtag people to further his mission of love in the world. I loved his unabashed desire to heal, feed, and love the least of these. Chills covered my skin as I read about his life. I was highlighting words left and right.

Around the same time, I also had a profound desire to join the Black gospel choir at my university. I tried out and, to my amazement, was accepted. Between my experiences of reading the gospels and the regular practices, prayers, and performances in various Black churches with the gospel choir, my heart was so full of love for Jesus. After a time of exploring religions, practices, and ways of worship, I had come back home to Christianity and was glad to be an intentional follower of Christ. I had never stopped loving him, but now I was in love with him. It felt different. Alive. Passionate. By my last semester in college, I was thinking about becoming a nun. I didn't understand what else I could be. My heart literally ached with the love of God in Christ. I loved the idea of being a nun; of being surrounded by other women who were in love with Jesus. There was just one problem with that idea. At twenty-one, I enjoyed dating, and I knew that one day I wanted a husband and children.

It's funny to look back and wonder why it wasn't more obvious that I could be a priest, particularly in the Episcopal Church, where women could be ordained, marry, and have a family. But it wasn't obvious. It never occurred to me until a few weeks after college, when I received an unforgettable call to become a priest in the Episcopal Church. I was sitting in the pew one Sunday, less than a month after I graduated from college, and the rector began his sermon with the words, "Why are you here?" He asked it twice. And then I began to hear God speak to me in my heart very clearly, telling me to imagine myself in the priest's shoes. I didn't understand at first. I looked nothing like the priests I was used to. I liked mascara and dating and painting my nails. I asked for another sign to confirm that what I thought I was hearing was accurate. Days later, I had a dream of a church procession. I was wearing a white robe. I was trying to be a helpful acolyte, carrying a candle but the job was taken. I offered to carry the cross, but someone was doing that too. The head acolyte was my beloved Brazilian godfather. He looked at me and said, "Your job is to be the last one in the procession, carrying nothing." I woke up and told my mom my dream, and she confirmed that the priest is the last one in the procession. It began to make sense—how I could live out this love of Christ and have the family I'd always dreamed of. I entered seminary at the age of 21 and was ordained in the Episcopal Church at 24. I was glad I didn't have a boyfriend at the time because, in my mind and heart, my ordination, which included lifelong vows, was akin to a marriage service to God. The lifelong seeking after God and the lifelong belief in the magical and mystical had been fulfilled in my ordination. I was exactly where I was meant to be.

I had been an Episcopal priest for over ten years when I endured a traumatic ordeal that formed cracks in my tender heart, preceding the day that my faith in the church was shattered by a phone call with the bishop. For a period of several weeks, I was sexually harassed by the rector at the Episcopal church where I served under him as an associate rector. His manipulations to be alone with me, his unwanted touches, and the offensive things he said made me feel like prey, constantly pursued by a larger and wilier predator. I would try to avoid him without angering him, but he would use his power to find times to be alone with me. In our large church, several priests led worship multiple times a week in a few worship spaces in a large, beautiful campus. I'm intelligent, and yet in the midst of this trauma, I felt outsmarted at every turn. He would show up when I was meant to be leading a service alone, or he would switch schedules with a colleague to be alone with me in the sacristy. He was not someone you wanted to anger, and I felt powerless. It was nightmarish. I didn't feel safe in the very place that had previously been my refuge and purpose. I got used to a constant undercurrent of anxiety, of feeling on edge, wondering every time I entered a room if I would find him there, waiting for me with ill intentions.

One Wednesday, I was supposed to be leading a mid-week worship service by myself. I enjoyed the quiet service with a few faithful parishioners. It was a perfect pause in the midst of very busy days, and I could temporarily forget my cares in the liturgical flow of Holy Eucharist. I looked forward to meeting each person's eyes at the altar rail, as I touched each warm hand with a communion wafer. I felt honored to be able to offer healing prayers at the altar to anyone who came forward. At the end of the service, I enjoyed sweet exchanges with the small group of parishioners, the light from the stained glass dancing in their eyes. After the last parishioner left, I returned to the sacristy as usual, only to find him in the vesting room nearby, his back toward me, waiting for me to enter the room where I would remove my vestments. The warmth and joy of the service drained from me, replaced by dread. I knew that verbal and physical harassment awaited me. Before he could turn around, I fled right past the vesting room and around the corner, to a private bathroom, quickly pulled my hair back, leaned forward to protect my vestments, and vomited in the sink. I gathered myself together and retreated to my office, still wearing my vestments, closer to where other staff would be, safe from harm.

There were many other times I could not escape harm. Since he didn't respect "no," nor seek my consent, I tried other ways, including appealing to the honor and integrity I assumed he must value as an ordained priest of God. After he heard me preach a sermon for a wedding and speak fondly of the love of two people in a marriage, I was sure that he would leave me alone. He didn't. I spoke often of the fact that Bryson, my husband, and I were engaged in a long process of approval to adopt a baby girl. I kept framed photos of my husband and boys at my desk. I was naïve enough to think that he would get the hint that our family was solid and didn't deserve harm at the hands of an outsider. He didn't care. He was always one step ahead of me, making escape feel impossible.

When it was my day to do hospital visits, he would announce that he would be accompanying me. He would check the worship schedule to see where I'd be on our large church campus and then show up there. It seemed like a game to him. This behavior, which made me feel like I was being hunted, went far beyond inappropriate comments, but that happened too. The unwanted physical advances were the worst. He forced his mouth to mine against my will. One time he pushed me up against a wall, knocking my head hard against the concrete. This was more than harassment. It felt like assault. I didn't know what gaslighting was back then, but he was a master at it. If I tried to avoid him accompanying me for hospital visits, he would either get very angry or insinuate that I was not able to do my job. I never wanted his anger to be directed at me, but the underlying threat was always there. I'd seen him fire people without remorse and make staff cry. He was a master at manipulation and deceit, and it was hard for me to understand how I could get out from under his manipulations without angering him, but I was determined to find a way. To the average parishioner, he was a well-liked, competent, and successful priest running a large church, but he was an abuser of power when no one was looking. I loved the people in that church, and I needed that job. My family needed the income and the health insurance. It wasn't easy to just find another job as an Episcopal priest. I had a good, solid, happy marriage with two young boys who attended the church preschool. Everything was right about where I was except for him, except for this awful situation that loomed over everything. I was haunted by what he told me clearly, on more than one occasion: "If you ever report my actions, I will just say it was consensual." In our hierarchical church structure, I had no doubt that he, in his position of authority at a large parish, would be believed over me, unless I had proof. Despite the fact that I knew I had done nothing to encourage him, I felt incredible shame about what he was doing to me— his words and actions. I could see no way out of this situation. I was well and truly trapped. And to think, a long time ago, I used to be a fighter.

The Spirit of a Warrior

For at least ten years of my childhood, I took karate. Karate was always about more than just fighting. My sensei taught us about the values that came with it such as honor and integrity. It was about protection, but it was also an art form, and he instilled in us pride in our movements. I was confident and capable when I was sparring, which was how we fought in karate by only exchanging light kicks or punches. I was quick to block a punch and swift in my movements. Once in a while we would gear up for a big weekend competition in a nearby city. During these competitions, girls only sparred with other girls. Except for me. I was considered such a tough fighter that they bent the rules to allow me to fight the boys. I would confidently look my opponent straight in the eyes, a ten-year-old warrior in a ponytail. I had no doubt that I could defeat my opponents, even if they were larger boys. I was assertive and focused on the discipline of sparring and my goal of winning. I came home with several trophies topped by a gold figure of a girl in a ponytail. She looked like me. I suspect I was also passionate about karate because it was the only sport I could do. I was born with a degenerative foot condition and have worn orthotics since I was a child. I still remember the day that the podiatrist told my mom right in front of me that not only should I never run and never play school sports, but that I would probably be in a wheelchair by the time I was forty. Karate didn't require running and yet awarded me for my passion and drive.

Over the years, though, my warrior spirit was subdued. It was replaced with typical societal conditioning for girls and women to be nice and please others. Both as a Latina and a girl raised in the South (in the Bible Belt of the United States, no less), I learned that any decent girl needed to be good and helpful. Helpful with tidying up around the house. Helpful with dinner—with chopping food, cooking, and setting the table. Helpful with clearing the table. Offering a cold drink to visitors. As the oldest sibling

I was helpful with my siblings. I couldn't see at the time that my sense of self-worth began to be tied to being of assistance to others. I found great meaning in assisting, serving, and helping others. In fact, my first job when I was 15 was as a waitress, where I got to serve others. I'm grateful for these values, except that, over time, I realized that I never put my needs first.

I'm sure my warrior spirit was also subdued because of what happened to me in high school. I was waiting to be picked up from an after-school activity and I was in the hallway with a good-looking older boy who was a popular football player. We had mutual friends but I didn't know him well. We were talking a little, when all of a sudden, he shoved me up against the wall right by the entrance of our school with my wrists pinned against the cold concrete. I have blocked the words he said to me even though he was inches away from me. It was unexpected and I was in total shock. I'd never experienced such force. He laughed off what he did, and I thought it was a bad attempt at flirting. A few days later, I went to a church youth conference and one of the adults saw the bruises on my wrists. She kept pushing me to tell her what happened. When I did, she said I needed to go to the principal. I really didn't want to because I knew if the boy got in trouble I would be blamed, but she insisted I report what happened to me. She drove me to the school, walked with me into the office, and listened while I told the principal everything. The principal saw my bruises. The popular football player got two weeks of detention, which included missing a big game. He told people that it was my fault he was suspended. As a result, a few students blamed me for my high school losing the big game. I still recall the penetrating glares and comments made to me in the student parking lot. I felt humiliated and embarrassed and wished I could have lied about what happened to me. Standing up for what was right didn't feel worth it to me at the time. Looking back, that was the end of it. I never went to therapy; I can't even remember if I told my parents about it.

Years later, I didn't understand the sexual harassment I faced in the church unlocked a state of active trauma going all the way back to this earlier experience in high school. I didn't understand that my physical sensation of being trapped and unable to go forward stemmed from my fear of suffering ramifications similar to those I'd faced in high school. I didn't understand that a previous encounter of physical harassment and harm, left unhealed and unprocessed, meant that I had a much higher chance of it happening again, that perpetrators have a way of identifying victims. I would later learn these things in therapy, along with the fact that my trauma responses, which ran the gamut from fight or flight to freeze or fawn, were normal and typical. Fawning was acting normal—like he wasn't harming me so that I wouldn't anger him. I most often responded by freezing because I felt trapped. I knew the consequences if I reported him. The rector had made it clear he would just say it was consensual, and I knew he would be believed. Going forward and speaking up in high school meant being blamed and shamed by a few teens. I would soon find out that it was far worse with adults in the church.

The Phone Call

My warrior spirit may have left me, but no part of me wanted what was happening to me. Fortunately, several weeks into the harassment, he sent me an email threatening my job if I were to ever go forward in reporting him. I finally had a way out. I contacted the office of the assistant bishop, a woman. Since I finally had evidence in writing, I felt sure that I would be believed, and justice would follow. The Episcopal Church has a hierarchical structure of authority, not unlike the Roman Catholic Church. A bishop oversees the diocese, which is a large region of land (and in some cases, the whole state). All Episcopal churches and the clergy working there are under the authority of the bishop. When the time came for me to meet with the diocesan bishop, he asked me if I would consider another option besides moving forward officially in a canonical process, which would likely include a church trial. He had spoken to the rector, and the rector agreed that he would leave me alone if I agreed to continue working there under him. I didn't hesitate in saying absolutely not. I could never go back to working for this man, and I knew that I would not be safe if I did. With that, the church trial began. I never could have imagined that this canonical process would be as traumatic as the harassment itself.

When I began seeing my therapist again in the midst of all of this, she didn't mince words. I was naïve enough to believe that after I came forward with the truth and evidence, this situation would end with me being believed and fully supported. But my therapist told me about another female minister client of hers who was "crucified" when she came forward in her church with a clear case of harassment. My therapist told me, "Churches are unable to handle the truth, Chantal, and they will blame you. This will not end well." She was exactly right.

There were many aspects of how the process unfolded that were excruciating for me. There was an initial attempt to keep confidential that I was the one that reported the rector, in hopes that I might be able to continue serving at that church. Once the trial process began, he was forbidden to come to the church. However, I struggled to do my job amidst an actual witch hunt. Before it was public knowledge that I was the one who had reported him, parishioners of power and prestige poured into my office, demanding to know who would do this to their rector. And then clergy who were tasked with holding this information in confidence in order to provide pastoral care to the staff were sloppy with their communication and shared my name with others. Word got out. The fingers were pointed at me now. But the most painful part of it all was yet to come. A date was set where the bishop, the canon to the ordinary,[2] and other representatives from the diocese would come to a large meeting at my church where hundreds of parishioners were invited to hear about the canonical trial[3] that would soon be taking place. This meeting was not the trial itself, and I was told that the hundreds of people gathered at the church would learn that there would be no trial since the bishop had already issued an order stating that the rector would be barred from serving as an Episcopal priest for a year. Essentially, the bishop had already decided the rector was guilty without the formality of a trial. Upon reading the order, I felt immense relief and hope that soon my life would resume some sense of normalcy. I was sure that once everyone heard this news, the witch hunt would end. Except that it didn't happen that way at all.

Then came that phone call that left me sobbing on my bedroom floor. In the hours before the large church gathering, the bishop explained that it was almost unheard of for a bishop's order to be challenged, but in this case the senior priest's attorney had rejected the order, which meant the matter had to go forward to a trial. My bishop told me this meant he had to portray both sides equally, as though he didn't know that I had been sexually harassed. He would say only that I described what took place as sexual harassment, and the senior pastor described it as consensual. I started shaking. I was in shock, crying, pleading with the bishop. "But you know! You have written proof! Why would you act as though you don't know the truth in front of hundreds of parishioners? I'm married with two young boys! You know I didn't want this!" But he said there was nothing he could do, that these were the rules of the canonical trial. This was what justice looked like, at this stage. It felt like he had punched me in the gut. I fell to the floor, heartbroken, stripped of dignity, and beyond shamed.

I was not at that church meeting, but I was told it was ugly. I was blamed for it all. The large church was packed with several hundred people, mostly parishioners and also some colleagues from area towns and cities. A parishioner stood up to proclaim that I must have "asked" for it. An older man blamed me for what I wore, despite the fact that I wore professional, modest clothing appropriate for a married priest in the Bible Belt. No one stood up for me when the accusations began. Not the congregants whose weddings and baptisms I had joyfully celebrated, not the parishioners who knew me from church committees, not even the bishop who knew the truth of what had happened. Although I learned later that there were people in the audience who supported me in spirit, the loud ones in the meeting were the ones blaming and judging me. Out of all the people I had served and served with for years, not one person stood up to defend me.

It just so happened that I had an appointment with another mental health provider the next day. I was crying so hard I could barely talk. "I feel paranoid," I said. "I was told that this was going to be over because they knew I was harassed but that's not what happened at all!" I showed him the copy of the order I was given and explained what happened instead. After he read it, he looked at me soberly and told me that I wasn't alone. He said this happened to a lot of women and a lot of people in the church. This was a pattern. A long, strong, ongoing pattern of abuse and protecting the abusers. He explained that he had a lot of experience working with abusers and the abused in the Roman Catholic Church, but this abuse happened in other denominations too; it just wasn't being talked about as much. He wasn't surprised at all. Although I felt paranoid to the degree that I was beginning to feel physically ill, it wasn't actually paranoia I was experiencing, he explained, because my deep mistrust was not unfounded. That sense of people being out to get me was my body's natural reaction to how this was unfolding. My very being was making sure I knew that I was not safe.

After the church meeting where hundreds of people were present, I couldn't even go to the local grocery store. I would be picking out produce for dinner and church members would give me disgusted looks and walk away. People glared at me. On occasion, someone would hug me by the oranges with a look of pity on their face, and I'd break down in tears and couldn't continue shopping. I was ordered by the bishop to be silent about the canonical proceedings for many weeks, which meant that I was not allowed to stand up for myself. In a hierarchical church culture, a priest takes orders from the bishop, and the bishop had silenced me. Even though the bishop had written proof of my harassment, and the church leadership was shown evidence of this as well, I was treated as a guilty party. I was told that the senior warden, the lay leader now in charge of the church in the rector's absence, decided that I was not allowed on church property. My two young boys had been going to preschool there, but I was no longer able to pick them up in the drive-through pickup line. Why? Attorneys explained to me it was because my church wanted to be portrayed as the victim in all of this. They didn't want the legal or moral responsibility that comes with workplace sexual harassment, knowing that I could file a Title VII complaint. Rather than show care to me, they preferred the optics of a consensual behavior scenario that justified their getting rid of not just the harasser but the one who was harassed. I faced rejection and judgement in real life and on social media from countless parishioners and colleagues. I was well liked and respected among my clergy colleagues in the diocese, but only one of them reached out to me, and that was to say that he was praying for both me and the rector, the one who harmed me. I felt that I had crossed an invisible line by openly saying something that could make the church look bad. The way the church looked in all of this was the only thing that mattered. Not the truth. Not even that I was being harmed. I was having anxiety attacks daily and wondered if my life could recover from such a downfall. An ordained minister has to have their integrity and dignity in order to function as a trusted leader of the faith, and now I had neither.

During this time, I practiced self-compassion by driving to the other side of town to shop at an international grocery store, one particularly frequented by Latinos. I'd shop for the comfort food I was raised with: tortillas and beans, cilantro, chorizo, and salsas, while being surrounded by the brown skin of my ancestors. I'd remind myself that many of them had experienced greater suffering than me. Some were refugees; some had escaped drug-ravaged towns with gangs. Surely some of the women had experienced worse treatment at the hands of a man. And there they were, shopping without tears, their children pulling their legs for candy. One day. One day I would get through this.

After the canonical trial took place, a panel determined that I had been sexually harassed, but the bishop said he could not call it that. Even though psychiatric reports backed up that finding, in addition to the email in which the rector had threatened my job. Even though a doctor, a lawyer, and a mental health practitioner all told me I could actually press charges for assault. In a letter to the hundreds of parishioners at my church, the bishop cited the canonical (church) law in a numerical code that referenced the violation for misconduct of a priest and the senior priest was "inhibited" for one year, which meant that he could not function as a priest for this short period. Without naming how the priest harmed me, the numerical code was surely meaningless to the vast majority of the congregation. The diocese acknowledged that I "was and had always been a priest in good standing," which was their way of acknowledging there was nothing consensual about the way he harmed me, and said they would support my healing. Yet at the same time, the bishop told me I needed to apologize in a letter to the church and also that I could not return because the gossip about me was so widespread and harmful to my integrity as a leader. I didn't know what I should be apologizing for, so he suggested that I apologize for reaching out to an employment lawyer when I was scared and needed an advocate shortly before I reached out to the assistant bishop.

I was brokenhearted to leave this church. I was brokenhearted by the reaction from clergy colleagues, staff members, and parishioners. I felt like a leper. The church itself made no effort to express compassion, regret, or sorrow at what I had experienced. There were some individual efforts quietly made. I had the unconditional support of my husband and family. One woman brought a stack of beautifully illustrated children's Christmas books for the boys and made sure I knew she was praying for me. One neighbor who was also a member of the church brought the boys' favorite meal, fried chicken and sides, for dinner after seeing us on a walk several months later. Two older men reached out who were in such shock from that church meeting that I ended up pastoring them. A few parishioners in their 30s, around my age, left the church after immediately recognizing how wrong it all was. Over the years, they have become dear friends who knew me at my worst. And then there were the letters. Handwritten letters, primarily from women in the church, began trickling in. They all expressed deep sorrow at what transpired, and many acknowledged that *they knew* even though the bishop's letter was vague. One moving letter was written by a woman who I guessed to be in her 80s. She advised me to move out of town and start over because it would never work for me to stay after what I'd been through. She knew because something similar had happened to her. While she didn't go into detail, I believe she meant she was accused of having an affair, when in fact she had experienced sexual assault/harassment. These letters showed me that, while what I went through was much more public than usual, it was not unknown to women. I wrapped the stack of letters in a rubber band and tucked them away for a day I might need the reminder that some people could see through the lack of transparency from the church.

While these private expressions of compassion and support meant so much to me, the church, the body of Christ that I had faithfully served for years, turned a cold shoulder. When a woman speaks out about harm being done within the church, there is often no result other than rejection. It broke my heart. Nighttime was the worst. In the quiet, the reality of my life settled in. I would lay in bed and the tears would form. I would then close my eyes and imagine a field of grass with Jesus sitting under a tree just ahead of where I was. Like a child, I would run to him and crawl into his lap and cry. I would cry like a little girl in his arms, as he comforted me with patience and quiet wisdom. He knew my heart. He knew my soul. He didn't judge me, and I didn't have to explain. I fell asleep with this vision every night for months. It was the only thing that comforted me enough to allow me to sleep. Yet every time I woke up, the weight of what was happening to me would hit me again and I would brace for another day.

And yet it still wasn't over for me. I had been officially diagnosed with PTSD, had begun intense therapy and medication, and had been approved for short-term disability. Still, the diocese sent me to yet another psychologist to confirm my diagnosis. Within a short time, she expressed confusion about why I was seeing her. "It's obvious that you were harassed, and the diagnosis is correct. If they think I'm going to disagree with the other mental health providers, they are wrong." She sent her report to the diocese. The diocese then said I needed to see a third psychologist. This time I had to leave my family and fly out of state to a center that focused on clergy misconduct in the Roman Catholic Church. I sat through hours of psychological testing. After all the testing was concluded, the psychologist said she didn't understand why I had been sent there. After I told her my story and showed her the order that never became public, she was silent for some time, putting all the pieces together, and then said she knew what she had to do. She said, "You need to see some transparency, so you will be present as I make a call to the diocese." When the canon to the ordinary was on speaker phone, she told him that the diocese was preventing me from healing by sending me from one psychologist to the next psychologist. "We are all saying the same thing. You are furthering her trauma and this needs to stop, now. You should not send her anywhere else. Can you commit to this?" He acknowledged what she said. He made an offhanded comment about how I should have said "no" to my abuser earlier and reported it earlier, and she corrected him by saying that it was actually quite astounding that I had come forward as quickly as I had. "It took Anita Hill years to come forward. It took Chantal only a matter of weeks and as soon as she had proof, she came forward. Shame and trauma prevent people from speaking up and coming forward sooner." At one point on the call, she asked what I thought, and I said, "I'm glad to see someone speaking truth to power." I couldn't fully see it at the time, but I now believe they kept sending me to psychologists to try to find just one mental health provider who would either say that the harassment was consensual so that the diocese wouldn't be held liable, or that I was mentally unwell so that they wouldn't have to find another church for me. What was apparent, either way, was that these repeated examinations had little to do with supporting my healing.

I flew back home in a state of despair. The sexual harassment itself had been traumatic, but it had been exacerbated by the canonical process, a church meeting with hundreds of people that was described to me as a witch trial, rejection from parishioners in the community, and repeated conversations about it with psychologists. When would this all stop? My God, I was in bad shape. It became clear to me that the diocese was treating me as a liability rather than as one who had been harmed. In the last few months, the culmination of all of this meant that I had become increasingly consumed with fear, shame, paranoia, and a deep distrust of the church.

When a person is cared for appropriately, they are nourished with love and compassion, and they thrive, like a plant growing under warm sunlight. But I felt like the compost rotting in our garden at the end of summer, the smell putrid in the heat, worms crawling through black sludge while everything rotted. I was rejected by parishioners I once visited in hospitals, parishioners whose babies I baptized, and parishioners I served on church committees with. I needed solidarity but I got looks of disdain wherever I went. Clergy colleagues who knew me for years turned a blind eye and went silent. Staff members who acknowledged to the diocese that the rector was a bully joined the crowds in rejecting me on social media and in real life. I once had a warm relationship with many in the church but discovered I was unfollowed and unfriended, while multiple comments were made about the church being the victim, as though my intention had been to harm the church. After coming forward with the truth, I was treated like I was rotten compost. It felt like I was disgusting to everyone who saw me.

Chapter 1
Reflection Questions

In solidarity with those who have experienced harm at the hands of another, the first set of questions are to support people who have been harmed and are on a journey of healing.

- How did you feel safe, encouraged, and free to tell the truth?
- If you experienced pressure to keep things secret, what did that look like?
- How did you experience or observe compassion?
- Where did you experience or witness ample care and concern once others knew of the harm you experienced?
- Did you experience shame or blame? If so, where did those feelings come from?
- Did you feel scapegoated? If so, explain.

These questions are to support the reader's ongoing solidarity with those who have been harmed:

- When have you been part of a faith community, job, or situation where you suspect or know that someone was harmed?
- Did you feel like you could reach out in support? If not, why not?
- What are some ways that you or others could show support, both privately and publicly, to a person who has been harmed by another person?
- How would speaking up alongside another friend or colleague help both you and the person who was harmed?
- In what ways did Jesus show solidarity to those who have experienced harm and suffering?

2

When You Stand Up for Justice, the World Will Rise to Meet You

I had never been so weak, so low, or so shamed. Yet in my weakness, I heard a still small voice, repeating to me: "When you stand up for justice, the world will rise to meet you." Again and again, I heard: "When you stand up for justice, the world will rise to meet you." And yet I felt exhausted and unable to stand. I was worn down by all of it, and I was in a place of trauma. I needed medication just to get through the day. The gossip was relentless. The way I was being treated was debilitating.

It seemed like I would be stuck in this place forever, and then God moved through my husband. My husband was raised on a North Carolina farm by family that loved Jesus and gave their life to the church. He is a man of honor and integrity. And at this point he'd seen enough. "It's time to speak up," he told me. "This isn't right. You have to, Chantal." My only response was more tears. I felt so weak that I couldn't possibly do what he was asking. But he persisted. "You have to speak up; I'll go with you." And he, who was also hurting, confused, and angry at the church, went with me to speak with the bishop and the senior warden about bringing this painful chapter to a close. I was beginning to stand up for myself, even as my knees were shaking.

During this time, I had one prayer that was my foundation. It was a prayer that my Mexican abuelita (grandmother) taught me as a teen. She did not have much formal education, but she had a profound spiritual faith. She was always reading Scripture and devotions and receiving insights about God that she couldn't wait to share with whoever was nearby. I can still hear her say these words, in her accent, her heart bright and full of wisdom:

"*Mi'ja*,[4] let me teach you a powerful prayer. Whenever you need clarity about something, pray that your eyes see the situation as Christ sees it. Pray that your heart loves people as Christ's heart loves them. When you don't understand something, pray that your understanding be the same as Christ's understanding. This is so powerful! *Pero*, be careful because this will change you, *mi hija*. It will change the way you see things. Try it, Chantalita."

And I did. I needed that prayer. I was wary of people in the diocese. I was wary of churchgoers. I was wary of colleagues who looked away and parishioners who judged me at the store. I wasn't sure if there was room for me in the church anymore. And my abuelita was right. That prayer transformed me. It allowed me to see that, while Jesus sees all things, people do not. It allowed me to see how parishioners were unable to fully understand what happened when the truth was not clearly shared with them, and they judged me with limited knowing. It allowed me to see that, because a hierarchical church relies on protecting and perpetuating itself, many people experience harm in the wake of the business of institutional religion. The church could get back to business as usual more quickly by treating me as a guilty party.

My abuelita's prayer allowed me to see how those in the Christian church often turn away from opportunities right in front of them to reach out in loving compassion. It's much more comfortable to serve those in need when we call it an outreach ministry, when those we help can remain largely anonymous or kept at a remove, a programmed, sanitized, colonized version of *loving one another*. I know because I was "othered" in the witch trial at the church where I served. I know because I was "othered" at the grocery store and around town. The abuse I endured was ugly to look at. To care for me would have been a reminder that the abuser, the one who harmed and threatened me, was their priest too. Toxic purity culture combined with misogyny in churches means that Christians are more likely to look away from and judge the many women who experience harassment and assault, rather than care for us with compassion. Over time, the Christ eyes I prayed for allowed me to more clearly see why people were anything other than compassionate. It still hurt, but at least I understood it better. The Christ eyes I prayed for also allowed me to see that the diocese was treating me as a liability, rather than one who could be trusted, and it was up to me to change their perspective.

Seeing with Christ's Eyes

After the third psychologist told them that these repeated psychological assessments needed to stop, one more meeting took place between the bishop, the canon to the ordinary, and me. I drove to the meeting with my hands tightly gripping the steering wheel as I prayed for God to guide my every word. I was still in bad shape, and I was distrustful, with good reason. But my ego had been shattered. My heart had been broken because of everything that had transpired. I had seen such an ugly side of the church I loved so much, both in the harassment and in how I was treated when I spoke up about it. I wasn't sure if I belonged there anymore. Yet I had nothing to lose, and strangely, that was liberating. I was tired of being treated as a liability. I was tired of not being trusted when I was actually the one who had come forward with a hard truth.

I said to the bishop, "I am not your enemy. I don't want to sue the church. I don't want one penny of the church's money. I want to be healed! I want you to support my healing and walk with me. I want to get back on my feet and serve the church as I have faithfully done for years!" He acknowledged that it had been an awful canonical process and that I had done my best in a terrible situation. He said he knew I had been harmed. Yet I could still feel that I was regarded with caution rather than care. Tears rolled down my red, blotchy cheeks. "I love our church because we believe in justice! We value justice for immigrants. We stand for racial reconciliation. We seek justice for the LGBTQ community. I've been active in leadership roles in our diocese for the sake of justice. But it's *my* turn now." My passion was rising in me, like a roaring flame. "It's *my* turn! Where is MY justice? I'm right here! It's time for my justice," I pleaded.

And in that moment, the energy in the room changed. Just like that, he saw me. He saw my heart. His energy changed. He believed my intentions, and he blessed me with these words. He peered into my tear-filled eyes, paused, and spoke slowly and sincerely: "I see you... I SEE you! You know, most of my priests are priests of the church. But *you*...you are *God's priest*. And today, I want to thank you for being a priest to me. Thank you. I see you, and I believe you." He finally saw me—with Christ's eyes.

Upside-Down Christ Eyes

Nine years after this trauma, I was invited to speak at a national conference for women clergy. I was there to share what it was like to serve as a woman clergy outside of the church. The planners of the conference asked me to speak about the journey that had led me to now serve outside of the church, rather than as a priest within the church. This meant I needed to name what happened to me, name the canonical trial and trauma that took place, and then move toward how I partner with church leaders to impact local communities and churches now. My knees were shaking behind the lectern. Even years later, speaking in front of women who would surely be supportive, I feared that my voice would quiver as I recalled the hardship of what I went through. But my voice remained strong as I shared how a year or so after my short-term disability ended, while serving part-time at a small rural parish, I began my first steps in manifesting the dream God had placed on my heart to become a church planter for a new church for working class and lower-income folks. Spending so much time with people often on the margins felt important to my healing and brought back memories from my childhood.

My parents and the church of my childhood instilled in me a deep love for those who are typically rejected by everyday society, which often includes white mainstream churches. In middle school, I often went to the local soup kitchen, Our Father's Table, to volunteer on Saturdays when I was with my Dad. I loved bringing the men, many of whom had no housing and struggled with addiction or mental illness, their meal; often soup, a roll, chicken and gravy, and a vegetable, all on a compartmentalized plate. Eventually I could greet them all by name. I prepared meals for people living with AIDS with my youth group and visited halfway houses with my Mom. Yet over the years, as a priest in the church, I was less and less able to spend hands-on time with people who were outcast or rejected. The responsibilities of parish priests are primarily focused on our parishioners. I spoke about service from the pulpit, and I visited church members in hospitals and retirement centers, but most of my time was taken by responsibilities inside the church building.

Now, after I had experienced firsthand what it felt like to be rejected, I was passionate about directly serving among those who had also been rejected. I wanted to start a church with them and be a priest with and among people who had experienced suffering and hardship, like I had. I eventually left the sweet rural church to give all my energy to this new church plant with the full support of the diocese. After all the ups and downs of the last couple of years, when I felt unseen by the diocese, having their enthusiastic support felt deeply meaningful. After years of meeting neighbors in Section 8 housing, laundromats, and tiendas, our little church was thriving and growing. We partnered with our community to start the city's first bilingual food pantry, where crowds of people gathered for food, fellowship, and prayer. We hosted a conversation with sheriffs, police officers, and immigrants around the topic of domestic safety. We sought to be a healing presence to the community and over time, we helped to create a spirit of mutual trust and respect between the community and the church.

That profound scar, etched in my soul, has become like a portal—an opening for my Christ eyes. It shattered one worldview and opened up my ability to see deeper. My Christ eyes allowed me to see upside down. I had experienced such ugly actions within a church whose external beauty would take your breath away. Now, I was in a lower-income neighborhood, paying rent to use a small, plain church building, and yet the team of people that gathered together to develop this church, and the neighborhood around us, and the way God worked through us to sow seeds of love together in this community were the most beautiful witness to Christ I'd ever experienced. Starting this church with all the people involved, even on the diocesan level, was healing to my heart on many levels. We were participating in the reign of God—the reign of Love[5]—in our community.

I love my upside-down Christ eyes that came after my faith in the church was shattered. It was with these eyes that I later started a coaching and consulting organization for churches, Root Thrive Soar, to train and support churches to focus more of their time and resources to becoming the Love of God in their communities. I began speaking at conferences of church leaders and found great meaning in supporting the church while being outside of the church structure. At the same time, I was astounded by the kindred spirits I met in homes and public spaces outside of church, and I knew that God was just as active in the community as in the church building (and at times, even more so).

That day at the women's conference I stood at the microphone, looking out at women clergy from across the church: bishops, canons, and priests who had made vows to serve God like I had. I wondered if any of them had been through a similar hardship. In sharing my story, I named how traumatic that period of sexual harassment and the canonical trial had been for me. I wanted to tell my story as an example of the epidemic of misogyny, in hopes that my story would help other women know they weren't alone. I wanted current and future women bishops to see an example of a woman who had been harmed by another clergy yet had gone on to have a meaningful ministry, both inside and outside the church. I'd heard that many women, after reporting harm, harassment, or assault, were forced to move to another diocese even though they did nothing wrong and I wanted to convey that women like us, who reported harm, could be trusted as church leaders. I also wanted to point to a God that heals and restores the wounded and weary, and who makes a way out of no way.

Later that day, a woman who was a priest in my diocese at the time of the harassment approached me. She said that she had been horrified, years ago, by how everything unfolded. She said, "You know he harmed another woman before you, right?"

It was as though time stopped. I hadn't known. I was so stunned all I could do was listen with my mouth agape as she told me how she spoke to the bishop about how unjust it was that he was only barred from ministry for one year, but her words had obviously had no effect.

I left that conference in shock, my mind racing to re-process all that had happened in light of this new information. The bishop had known that another woman came forward about being harmed by this man when he allowed him to come to the church as the new rector where I was an associate priest. When he presented an option to have me go back to work under the rector with no trial and no discipline for him, the bishop knew he'd done this before. I remembered how hundreds of people had gathered at the church where I served for years to hear about the trial. When men stood up and yelled out, judging my character, and saying I must have asked for it, the bishop and his staff were quiet, despite knowing that I wasn't the first to report this man. When the church had banned me from setting foot on church property, the bishop told me there was nothing he could do about it, despite the fact that in the Episcopal Church, the diocese owns the property, not the parish. The bishop supported those decisions with full knowledge of this priest's history of harming women.

I also recalled how, in the beginning of the trial, the diocese told me that the rector was sent to a beautiful conference center on retreat for a few days, to allow him time to pray in hopes that he would agree that he was guilty. At the same time, I was taking daily medication to manage high anxiety and depression, and had to resort to asking for help with parenting my children while in a state of active trauma. I would have given anything to have a few days on retreat in a beautiful setting, away from the judgement of church folks. I now knew they had paid for his tranquil retreat knowing that he had harmed a woman before. I wondered if I would have received such harsh judgement from parishioners if the church had been told he had done this before and that the diocese had proof it was happening again. I then remembered how the diocese had me go to three different psychologists though they all agreed I'd been sexually harassed, harmed, and was in a state of active trauma. I thought about how my paranoid feelings about the diocese not prioritizing my well-being were exactly right after all, and how stunning it was that they would treat a woman who came forward the way they did, knowing it wasn't the first time. Nine years later, my mind raced through these unwelcome memories, my heart breaking all over again.

Once again, I prayed for Christ's eyes and Christ's heart to become my own. I prayed and I prayed. And slowly, with the confidence, clarity, and peace that only Christ's eyes and Christ's heart could bring, I began stepping back to see the scope of this problem. My Christ eyes became eagle eyes, allowing me to soar above my personal situation to embrace an eagle-eye view, a wider view, of the systemic harm that was happening in the church. This wider view caused me to further differentiate God from organized religion. I would not distance myself from the many, many people in churches who I had come to love and appreciate, who are the body of Christ. I would not lose hope in the concept of communities centered in following Christ. If anything, I was more passionate than ever about my desire to work with churches that wanted to learn how to be church in new ways. I was distancing myself from church-as-business. I prayed for Christ's eyes and Christ's heart, and I knew I would never allow any religious authority figure to come in between me and God again. I thought about how, over the years, those male clergy, including the rector, had all since risen to more prominent, higher positions of authority in our hierarchical church. Higher salaries, more titles, and more power. Meanwhile I, by choice, preferred my hands-on ministry with food pantries, sidewalks, jail, and the vibrant community around my church. I could not unsee what I had seen. My Christ eyes only further developed my vision in seeing corruption, lies, and misogyny. This also meant that it became more and more challenging for me to experience the pure love of God in church like I had before. I'd sit in pews, my stomach in knots, wondering how much of the pledge income of the good people I was sitting around would go up to the hierarchy to support hidden costs like liability issues, instead of out into the community. I wondered if they knew the extent to which their money supported things like repeated psychological testing for women who reported being harmed by a priest. Did they know their money supported retreats for the guilty and multiple modalities of care to support healing for the victim when there never should have been a repeated victim? Did they know that priest searches and bishop searches included men that were complicit in this cycle of harm, even as the church professed immense pride in valuing justice? The veil had been removed; the curtain had been pulled back. My Christ eyes were seeing more clearly than ever. I could not unsee that I had been harmed by more than one person in the church now; I had been harmed by the system of church-as-business; church-as-empire. My eagle-eye perspective with my wide-open Christ eyes led me to understand that I was not alone.

Chapter 2
Reflection Questions

- When have you stood up for justice?
- Identify a time when you were inspired by someone else who stood up for justice. Did others rise to meet them in the moment?
- Where do you tend to experience the movement of the Spirit of God—in the world or inside a church building? If you have experienced both, how is the movement different in the world from in the church?
- What thoughts and feelings arose in you when you learned that the man that harmed the author had also allegedly harmed another woman before, and the bishop allegedly knew all along?
- Name a situation that you would like to pray to have Christ's eyes about, so that you can see and understand the situation better.
- What is one thing you can do to ensure that injustice like this does not occur?

3

Confronting the Shadow Side of Church and Patriarchy with Christ Eyes

Perspective from a "Lost Sheep"

> *"What do you think? If a shepherd has a hundred sheep, and one of them has gone astray, does he not leave the ninety-nine on the mountains and go in search of the one that went astray? And if he finds it, truly I tell you, he rejoices over it more than over the ninety-nine that never went astray. So it is not the will of your Father in heaven that one of these little ones should be lost."*
> —MATTHEW 18:12–14

In the United States alone, 40 million people have left their church in the last 25 years.[6] That's a lot of "lost sheep," as those in the church would say as they shake their head at we who have "gone astray." But what is the church doing about the harm, pain, and trauma it has caused to its own people? A disease infecting the very system has slowly grown and is invading the culture of the church.

This disease is caused by a church culture that feeds off the duality of painting the church as pure and holy while at the same time hiding away the shadow sides of the church. Symptoms include: an exorbitant amount of time and financial resources spent fighting liability issues while covering up their own sin, a lack of transparency, an unwillingness to care for those harmed in the spirit that Christ would, and general atrophy, all while millions of members are leaving.

Unbeknownst to so many churchgoers, the patriarchal, institutional church operating in a capitalistic, consumeristic context is a money-making business. The church seeks to glorify God, even as protecting the image of the church to support membership and operating budget goals means that deceit and secrecy cover up unjust and harmful behavior. According to The National Catholic Reporter, between 2004 and 2023, "Catholic dioceses, eparchies, and men's religious communities spent more than $5 billion on allegations of sexual abuse of minors."[7] During this 20-year time frame there were more than 16,200 "credible allegations of sexual abuse by priests, deacons, or religious brothers."[8] The Southern Baptist Convention also covered up widespread sexual abuse. A report from 2022 revealed that "survivors who came forward alleging they were sexually abused by church leaders, ministers, workers, and volunteers were ignored or silenced by church leadership and often disparaged."[9] Yet at the same time, the Southern Baptist church maintained a secret list of more than 700 offenders. These are massive numbers, and yet they are just a few examples of church leadership and culture that supports a pattern of harm toward others that goes unseen.

The institutional church ends up protecting and enabling a cycle of harm toward women, children, and others, rather than transparently dealing with the problem, because covering it up protects the institution and keeps people in the pews and money flowing. This is systemic, not just a few bad apples. The system allows the bad apples to continue on, even advancing their leadership. To be clear, I believe the vast majority of people in the church are good people. Many clergy went to seminary like

I did, with a pure heart and a strong desire to serve God to the best of their abilities. Some are conflict-averse and become complicit in this system, looking the other way so as to not rock the boat. Even people with strong ideals and values can be afraid to speak up when no one has gone first. Yet this church system, as it stands, also attracts people with poor intentions and a history of bad behavior. The power and authority given to church leadership attracts some who abuse that power in the name of Christ. The culture of the church is infected with a systemic disease of harm that has not been adequately dealt with. It is a broken system that needs to be broken open. Is it beyond redemption by Christ? Of course not. Nothing is beyond God's redemptive abilities to restore and make anew. But to be redeemed, the church must fall to their knees in humility and sorrow, begging forgiveness from the millions of people who have experienced trauma there. The church must become like a child, learning new ways of being. The church must seek to reform and undergo a thorough process of disentangling itself from this disease which causes it to put the priorities of the church-as-business before the cause and compassion of Christ. This disease must be eradicated before institutional Christianity steps into the full potential of what its future could become. We cannot carry this disease of harm, violence, and misogyny with us into the future. The challenge, of course, is that this disease has festered for centuries.

Justo's Bones

> "And Moses took with him the bones of Joseph who had required a solemn oath of the Israelites, saying, 'God will surely take care of you, and you must carry my bones with you from here.'"
> —EXODUS 13:19

From the church's beginnings, we can find stories of oppression, violence, and even murder in the name of the church or to protect it. Years ago, my mom's cousin asked me if I ever wondered why our family had been Protestant for well over 100 years, even though our family was from Mexico. My cousin is our family historiographer and has explored detailed records of our ancestors, going back to the 16th century in Mexico. My great-grandfather, Sixto, was born in 1867 in Guadalajara, Mexico—a time and place of chronic instability. Sixto grew up poor and as a small child he sometimes slept in the alcoves of the great Guadalajara Cathedral, a historic Roman Catholic Cathedral originally built in 1541. As a kid, Sixto was a bone collector. He dug through the ancient catacombs of churches, carrying a burlap bag in search of bones and skeletons. He would sell what he found as the calcium in the bones was a key ingredient in the making of explosives. As my cousin, Rick, said, "explosive times required actual explosives."

Around the age of ten, deep beneath a church, Sixto found numerous skeletons of children, discarded in an undignified way and hidden amidst the catacombs. It was obvious to him that he had uncovered some mendacity going on within, and below, this place of worship. That day he did what he had to do. He filled up his bag and moved forward, but the burden of stumbling upon hundreds of children's skeletons eventually shattered Sixto's faith in the Roman Catholic Church. As an adult, after immigrating north to the United States in 1892, he eventually left the Roman Catholic church and changed his name to Justo, which means "justice." But before he left for the United States, he had yet another haunting encounter with bones at a religious site. At one point, Justo found himself doing bricklaying work in a Roman Catholic convent in Mexico, likely Jalisco. He discovered that several of the bricks were hollowed out. Rather than solid brick, they held the tiny skeletons of babies.[10] He couldn't be sure whose babies they were, but additional research has led me to suspect they were babies born to the nuns, potentially from sexual encounters that were not consensual. While his faith in the Catholic Church may have been shattered, he carried on with a stronger faith in Christ. He and his future wife, Mercedes (Mercy), also an immigrant from Jalisco, became Protestants and were both ordained in the Church of Christ. Because of his leadership qualities and fluency in three languages—Spanish, English, and Yaqui—Justo became a railroad foreman (not a typical job for a Mexican immigrant), and the expanding railroad sent Justo and Mercedes all over Southern California and parts of Arizona. At each place Justo was posted, they planted a Spanish-speaking Protestant church and ministered to the social and spiritual needs of the Mexican community. Justo was also an active voice for the Mexican community, using his experience and formidable powers of persuasion to advocate for justice and fair treatment for immigrants until his death in 1939. The horrors he uncovered as a child and young man only clarified his life's purpose and conviction to forge a new path as he followed Christ.

The story of Justo and the bones he found stays with me. The bones themselves could not be destroyed and lay there witnessing to the injustice that happened years before. The bones lay there, crying out, and my great-grandfather heard their cry. Dr. Clarissa Pinkola Estes, in *Women Who Run with the Wolves*, states that "the censoring ego most certainly wishes to forget it ever saw the room, ever saw the cadavers." And yet, like the naïve women she is describing, we cannot "end this process by pretending it is not occurring."[11] I tried for years to forget what I experienced, but my naïveté died with my trauma, and the wise woman in me was born of suffering, resolve, and a shattered worldview of church.

The story of Justo's bones has been passed on in my family through three generations. Pinkola Estes writes that "archetypally, bones represent that which can never be destroyed. Stories of bones are essentially about something in the psyche that is difficult to destroy. The only thing that we possess that is difficult to destroy is our soul."[12] I have no doubt that the souls of these bones have been crying out, insisting that their stories be told. Like them, those of us who have experienced harm may have been wounded, but our souls cannot be destroyed. We do have work to do: we must liberate our divinity from oppression. We must liberate our souls from the harm that we experienced. We cannot allow the egos of religious leaders to hide our stories, nor can we allow the naïve to pretend our stories don't exist. We must call out our truths and invite God to transform these shadows and accompany us to a new way. We have the strength of thousands of ancestors behind us. I know because I feel them.

Patriarchal Christianity's Long Pattern of Violence and Control

My great-grandfather's discovery mirrors the hundreds of children's skeletons found in 2017 in the Irish town of Tuam on the property of a Catholic religious community run by the Sisters of Bon Secours.[13] From the 1920s to the 60s, the Sisters of Bon Secours took in upwards of 60,000 babies and children from women who were unmarried when they got pregnant. Thousands of the babies were taken from their mothers, who were deemed "fallen women," and then adopted abroad, with money going to fund the Catholic Church. There was a BBC documentary about "the estimated 60,000 babies that the Catholic Church took for adoption in the 1950s and 1960s, many of them sent to America in return for large payments disguised as 'donations.'"[14] This is a crystal-clear example of how the church profits by shaming sex. Once again, we see an obvious example of the church's abusive past that still produces ripple effects. Consider how many people today are working toward healthier concepts of sexuality after experiencing shame from the church they grew up in, or worse, from the church they are currently a part of that shames natural expressions of sexuality or "illegitimate" children to conform to the church's image of what is good and holy. And yet, in this case, even worse than the church profiting from shaming sex is the overt mistreatment of innocent babies.

The babies were so mistreated and neglected that their mortality rate was astronomical. Three hundred infant deaths alone were reported at the workhouse between 1943 and 1946. In 1972, after the nuns sold the property, local children digging for worms for bait lifted up old slabs and found, to their horror, not worms but hundreds of babies' skeletons, nearly 800 in total, according to scholar Martin Sixsmith, author of the book *Philomena*, the story of one woman who was housed there, later made into a film starring Judi Dench.

These buried bones remind me of the unfathomable number of people whose lives were destroyed for the purposes of conversion to Christianity, from early missional efforts to the Crusades. Approximately one million people died in the first crusade alone. There are documented and graphic descriptions of the carnage. The Archbishop of Tyre, an eyewitness, wrote, "Everywhere lay fragments of human bodies, and the very ground was covered with the blood of the slain. It was not alone the spectacle of headless bodies and mutilated limbs strewn in all directions that roused the horror of all who looked upon them. Still more dreadful was it to gaze upon the victors themselves, dripping with blood from head to toe."[15] The history of how we spread our faith is permeated by a spirit of willful glee when violence is perpetrated against the enemy, who seemed to be anyone who was determined to be a threat to the church.

From 1484–1750, modern scholars believe that hundreds of thousands of women who were called witches (80% of all accused witches were women) were either burned at the stake or hanged.[16] By now you may not be surprised to learn that scholars now believe that witch trials allowed "Catholic and Protestant churches to compete with each other for followers" by effectively rallying membership and keeping women in line.[17] In fact, witch trials began after the Protestant Reformation. The church was now split into two factions, Catholic and Protestant, and they "used the attention-grabbing witch trials as perverse advertisements for their brand."[18] Once again, women were harmed while the church profited.

Anyone who spoke outside of orthodox Christian doctrine could be considered a heretic during the Inquisition, which began in the 12th century. The shadow side of the spread of Christianity includes harm toward not just women and children, but Jews, Muslims, Native American and Indigenous peoples, Africans and African-Americans, people called witches, and scientists who were poisoned, murdered, hanged, burned, beaten, or persecuted in violent ways in the name of the church. Inquisition courts were finally abolished in the early 19th century, but the genetic coding of such judgement and violence continues today.

And then there is the role of the church in the transatlantic slave trade. According to the Equal Justice Initiative, "Rooted in a belief that their duty to spread Christianity justified their actions, religious organizations not only embraced human trafficking and the enslavement of millions of Africans—they actively participated," beginning in the 15th century.[19] "Abduction, abuse, and enslavement" of nearly thirteen million Africans took place for nearly five centuries. Take a moment to conceive that nearly thirteen million people were enslaved to support, in part, the colonization of Christianity. The church benefitted in numerous ways and was in partnership with the state, once again leaving a legacy of suffering and trauma while the church benefitted. Do we really think we have purged ourselves from these atrocities? The Rev. Dr. Gayle Fisher-Stewart pointedly asks in her book, *Church Hurt*, "When did racism—America's apartheid—end? When did the Christian Church in these United States free itself from racism?"[20]

Interconnected with the slave trade is the genocide and land dispossession of Native Americans, instigated by the Doctrine of Discovery in the 15th century, which legally allowed European white nations to exploit and take over lands of non-Christians, and could harm and kill the people there with the blessing of the church.[21] But this atrocity did not end centuries ago. It lingered in the genetic coding of the church, a systemic disease slowly festering and growing.

According to the National Native American Boarding School Healing Coalition, "There were more than 523 government-funded, and often church-run, Indian boarding schools across the U.S. in the 19th and 20th centuries. Indian children were forcibly abducted by government agents, sent to school hundreds of miles away, and beaten, starved, or otherwise abused when they spoke their Native languages."[22] Once again, church-run entities took children from their parents and abused them while turning a profit.

These are just a few examples of the horrific abuses perpetrated by the church over its long history. It is impossible to cover every abuse in full, and yet we must understand the scope of the past with the perspective of an eagle and with the lens of Christ eyes in order to move forward. Lingering here matters.

It matters because colonization, misogyny, patriarchy, control, and fear still remain as symptoms of a disease deeply rooted in the church's genetic coding, present since the days of the Roman empire, yet drastically opposed to the teachings of Jesus.

In these examples, we see vestiges of empire that are woven through Christianity. While resistance movements have done much to support aligning the church with Christ's values, there is harm still happening beneath the surface. And any time individuals or groups of people are harmed, it is not faithful to Christ. Anytime the church harms another, it is a remnant of empire—and, needless to say, this is still very much a part of our culture today. So the question becomes, how does our faith rid itself of these vestiges of domination and harm, no matter how insidious it may be in our capitalistic, consumeristic, patriarchal context? These remnants of empire are harmful to Christianity and we must call it out and name it in order to move beyond it.

The perpetuation of harm cannot be carried forward into a future expression of church.

It is clear that we have not fully sought to move beyond our love affair with violence done to others in the name of God, so that the church may profit from an abuse of power, prestige, reputation, and wealth. In many cases, these are the values of the church that are hidden from the average Christian going to worship in a church on a Sunday morning. Just as humans' genetic coding determines much of who they are, these terrible parts of our history not only still exist in the Christian church today, they were part of its foundation. The church cannot make a sincere attempt to rid itself of the current injustice unless it goes back to examine its roots. Just as a person reflects on their family of origin in therapy, we must critically examine our past in order to shape the present and future we so desire. We, as followers of Jesus, must look to our often-hidden past to name the atrocities that were supported in the name of Christ in an effort to examine our present. And those of us who have experienced harm must support one another as we, together, stand up and tell our story. After all, these injustices of the past are very much a part of the present—they reverberate through our society today. Men who have harmed women have been elected as politicians, bishops, priests, and pastors. We must tell our stories—no matter how uncomfortable and ugly they are. We must tell the true story of what is happening in the present because we believe that a new way is possible. God is always ready to move through us to make a new creation. But we have to say "yes." We have to believe that God can make a way out of a wilderness full of abuse, trauma, and even bones.[23]

With the faith that God can do a new thing, let us carry the bones of the forgotten through this wilderness. I am inspired by Moses, who carried Joseph's bones to the Promised Land after Joseph said, *"God will surely take care of you, and you must carry my bones with you from here."* Let us honor the countless lives that ended in violence in the name of our Prince of Peace and walk with faith toward a way of following Jesus that feels like a new creation. But we won't forget the past. We won't allow secrets anymore. I carry the bones that Justo found in my heart. More than that, I appeal to those spirits, to the ancestors of the oppressed and to my ancestors, to strengthen our voice, our courage, and our conviction. Let us carry Justo's conviction for justice and his deep desire to forge a new path as he goes, with Christ by our side. We carry the bones, the stories, the souls of the millions of lives that ended in bloodshed. We lament that sharing the Good News was done in atrocious ways. We grieve that the teachings of Jesus were forced through violent ways. We carry the bones of those who have gone to their grave with secrets they were too ashamed to tell. We carry the knowledge that our historical past is part of a present pattern of injustice that needs to be broken open. I imagine Jesus weeps with us. I imagine him helping us carry these bones with us to a promised land we can't yet see. A land where the love of God is experienced with tenderness, vulnerability, and love. A land where living out the gospel through force, manipulation, and fear is archaic. A land where the reign of Love is experienced through peace and freedom for every being. With the help from Christ and our ancestors, we carry these bones toward that promised land.

Chapter 3
Reflection Questions

- Why do you think 40 million people have left their church in the last 25 years (15 million of them in the last 10 years)? What are some of the reasons?
- What is it like for you to consider separating your faith in the church from faith in Christ?
- Explore the many feelings that come with reading the shadow side of the history of the growth of Christianity. Where do you think we went wrong?
- Do you believe the ancestors of our faith hear our prayers and our lament?
- At this stage of the book, do you have hope in our future?

4

Burying the Seeds of Lament / I Will Not Walk Away from Jesus

LAMENTS: AN OFFERING FOR THE COMPOST PILE

Those bones represent old wrongdoings, but they are very much mirrored in our modern, collective laments about the church. What laments have been buried over the last two millennia and what is being buried today that yearns to be unearthed? Let us dig into the ground of history, uncovering and turning over our laments, tilling the soil for seeds of new life.

Why is it that we have extravagant bishops' consecrations that often cost six figures for one day? I lament these opulent celebrations of hierarchy while millions of households are scraping by, figuring out whether they can afford coats for their children and struggling to pay their utility bills. I lament that I partook at one of these consecrations while families living nearby experience hunger.

I lament that churches often spend tens of thousands of dollars on worship vestments while fentanyl is gripping our nation and people are resorting to selling harmful substances because they are desperate to feed themselves and their families. I lament that I have experienced the pride and inflated ego that comes with wearing regal chasubles.

I lament the hundreds of millions of dollars tied up in endowments and funds of many mainline denominations, so that the interest can primarily bless the institutional church. I lament the current system we have of putting the needs of the institutional church before following Jesus. I lament that I have surely benefited from this.

I lament excessive church capital campaigns that seek to raise millions of dollars to renovate buildings that often sit empty several days of the week. Such capital campaigns further strain income allocated outside of the church for the community in need. I lament that what is a practical need for churches does not often equate with a significant benefit for those living in poverty around the church. I lament that I have been part of this system.

I lament that the church turns away from the stories, the scars, and the trauma of the very people they have wounded. They turn away from the pain they caused, while prioritizing extravagant worship, beautiful church buildings, and growing their church-as-business. I lament that the actions of church leaders have made me feel unsafe and wary in the very church I love. I serve the church now on the margins.

I lament that I am not alone in what happened to me. I lament the countless stories I have heard from women in the church—many of whom are unemployed, underemployed, or on short-term disability like I once was. Women who struggle to thrive in our church as it exists now. I lament the experience of a woman who endured a culture of ongoing sexual harassment in a large Episcopal organization who tried to pursue justice but was told she had limited options because her harasser was not an ordained employee. I lament that she endured clear grooming, derogatory comments made publicly, and the silos that are formed when victims or harassed employees are pitted against one another. I lament that she left her organization for the repair of her soul only to have her writing stolen and published under the name of the very man who abused her. I lament that another woman told me she had been harassed by the same man, and yet other women have shared how harmful the culture of this organization has been toward them.

    I lament that our history of colonization benefits from dichotomies. The church codified and encouraged dichotomies. The church is good; the world is evil. Your sexual purity is good; sex is bad. Going to church on Sunday is good; non-churchgoers are selfish. The church understands God; the world does not, so you should doubt anything coming from people not in the church. God the Father was emphasized while Woman Wisdom (Sophia) was suppressed. The word of God from the pulpit is good; your intuition is bad. Ritual is only good inside a church; ritual outside of the church is done by witches. I lament that women who sought to live independently from church rules were persecuted and killed. They were called witches and painted with warts and wrinkled skin. Women's wisdom was mocked by calling their wrinkles ugly. Demean the women. Call them adulterers. Put them on trial. Judge them. Shame them. Kill them. I lament that to this day women are seen as second-class citizens in our own faith.

    I lament that for too long I conformed to the cookie-cutter shape of colonized church at the expense of allowing my full self to shine. On my Mexican side of my family, many have the gift of prophetic dreams and intuition. But there was no place in the church for that side of me to be welcomed and honored. There was no room for how God moves *in that way* in the church. I lament that I minimized myself to fit the mold of a church leader. Oh, how I wish that the cookie-cutter stereotypes of what faithful Christians look like could burn in a fire whose smoke rises, transmuting the confines that have limited us for too long!

    I lament that many people still struggle with the pain, grief, and anger from the harm their ancestors experienced in the name of God. I lament that many people now think God is angry and harmful due to the pattern of the church. I lament that so many people cannot make sense of the dissonance between words and action, between a church that seeks to be good, pure, and right, and yet so far has been unwilling to look at their own shadow side, their own sin, their own complicity in causing harm and trauma towards women. We see that the church has not yet been healed or transfigured from its own violent past. I lament that the church, overly concerned with an image of goodness and holiness, still continues the pattern of shame, secrecy, fear, and control that has been a part of its history.

I lament the deaths that still happen today on account of ongoing shame, caused by a culture of inflammatory judgement from Christians. Years ago, as a parish priest, I went to visit a man who was dying from lung cancer in his home. I was invited into the home by the man's lifelong partner. They were both active members of our church. The partner went upstairs and slowly carried his sick, frail partner in his arms, like a baby, down the steps, and gently placed him on the couch near where I was sitting. I watched as he carefully tucked a soft blanket around his thin body, adjusted the blinds to ensure there was no glaring light, and turned on his favorite classical music to play softly in the background. He left us to visit while he entered the kitchen to warm up some home-made soup. As I observed his compassionate care, I could hear the quiet voice of God say to me, "This is your example for love in sickness and in health. Never mind that they are not married.[24] Remember this moment." And I did. I was newly married and I took it all in, one part in awe at the gift of being able to witness such a pure, gentle, tender moment of love and another part of me bewildered at how people can't honor love that doesn't look like their own. The man with cancer died a short while later and it was an honor to assist at his memorial service. Tragically, later on, his partner, the one who so graciously showed me a glimpse of a spouse's unconditional love, took his own life. He left a note to the rector and me. Without his partner, he had no family. His family were conservative Christians who rejected him for loving his partner long ago. He loved our church but could not overcome the void of having no family. My heart was broken at how a man who so clearly modeled love and care for the sick could be rejected by his own flesh and blood, fellow Christians. I give thanks that the Episcopal Church and other denominations have advocated for justice and full inclusion, recognizing that Love is Love. Their solidarity toward LGBTQ people are seeds of hope for our future church. And, I lament the countless lives lost due to harsh rejection and judgement.

It is as though we have forgotten what Jesus' simple teachings are about. Parmahansa Yogananda said, "Jesus Christ was crucified once; but his teachings are crucified daily." I know this is true because I have been a part of the church that has participated in these daily crucifixions by way of judgement and condemnation of others, or worse, instilling shame and fear rather than dignity and worth. I lament that I, too, may have benefitted from the unknown pain inflicted on others. And I certainly have been wounded and scarred by these daily crucifixions. Creator, forgive us, for we know not what we do!

My spirit cannot make sense of how we have lost our way. I lament that we have institutionalized, made into tradition, and attempted to protect inside our church buildings the humble, authentic way of following Jesus. It has become programmatic (consumeristic in a way that primarily benefits those paying for the services), capitalized, and membership-oriented as the love of Christ stays inward more than outward into the community. The way of Jesus, however, cannot be contained, owned, or kept inside of any building.

I lament that this harm is not unique to Christianity, that Christianity is not the first or only faith where women's voices, wisdom, perspectives, stories, and leadership are not as respected as men's. I lament that, although every human was born from a woman, patriarchy has made women of the world second-class citizens in their religions too.

The Death of Nostalgia

I lament the death of nostalgia born from a limited perspective. I've met countless people that have had to reconcile sweet memories of Christmas pageants and potlucks with the reality that church-as-business has also harmed countless people and perpetuates shame and trauma. My wide-open Christ eyes can no longer pretend there isn't a massive shadow side to the church that has yet to be adequately brought to the surface so that the Christ light can shine and heal these untold stories.

And yet I have countless fond memories that stay with me. I've spent most of my life thus far in the church. I'll always have a place in my heart for church folk. I've been raised and nurtured by Sunday school teachers and acolyte leaders and by friends' parents in the church. I've been loved and supported by friends who were seminarians and professors. I've been mentored by priests and bishops. I've been encouraged and affirmed, and most importantly, I've collaborated in increasing God's love in the world with countless parishioners, both inside and outside of the church. I've been on the receiving end of prayers and casseroles delivered to my door when I had my babies. I have been present for the spectrum of life for hundreds of church folk: from blessing newborns to accompanying the dying as they transition—and I am always reminded of the good-heartedness of the vast majority of people I have met, whether in a food pantry line, a hospital, a homeless shelter, a graveside, or on a Sunday morning.

I'll always have a place in my heart for church folk. This makes sharing my story all the more difficult. Who wants to hear the inconvenient and painful truth that systemic misogyny and patriarchy in the church they love have harmed countless women? Who wants to actually know what a small percentage of their money directly blesses people in their community while the vast majority stays inside the church or goes up to the hierarchy? Who wants to know just how much of their bishops' time and diocesan funds are spent on liability issues? Or that church culture emphasizes the parts of the Bible that benefit the church, while conveniently de-emphasizing the parts that empower and strengthen your ability to directly hear the Word of God in your heart? This is not easy to hear, I know. I lament the death of sentimentality that comes from seeing a wider perspective with Christ-eyes.

A Secret System of Support for Women

I lament that this terrible legacy of secrecy that we have inherited keeps those who have been harmed from finding a support network, even today. As a result, even those people who want to work for a different way often must operate in secret in order to support women who have been harmed. I can attest to a system of support for women, consisting of individuals who are ready to quietly be in solidarity with women who have experienced pain, trauma, and abuse in the church. I lament the need for such a support system, but these individuals and the solidarity they offer are seeds of hope. They often function independently from one another and are not able to be vocal about this critical care they offer, for fear of retaliation. If a woman who is harmed is fortunate enough to have someone point her to one of these individuals, then she can reach out to receive prayers, solidarity, and emotional and practical support as she navigates the church system while reporting and/or experiencing harassment, abuse, emotional harm, retaliation, threats, and more. This support makes a huge difference to the well-being of the women who have been harmed as they live, work, and serve within patriarchal religion.

I lament that in so many cases, we who now support other women don't have a means of knowing who else is also sharing in this important work. I only know of this because I spoke at a women's conference about being harmed. And then, one by one, I began hearing from other women. What should be an organized network is fragmented. We function in silos because patriarchy doesn't value collaboration. We function in secret because patriarchy would never choose transparency of these shadows of harm still happening in the church. Yet I know of women and even some men who are part of these secret systems of support.

I am grateful to now be in a place where my own trauma is healed enough that I can accompany and support other women who reach out to me as they experience harm in the church. I know of other women who want to be able to provide support, but their scars are still healing, and hearing stories from other women is triggering. In my case, my husband knows that if I get a text or a call from a woman, I will step away from parenting for a little while so that I can be there for them in their time of crisis. I have had multiple conversations with women who have experienced all forms of verbal, emotional, and sexual harassment and abuse, as well as retaliation. I would have given anything to have experienced support from a woman who had experienced harm in the church when I was at my worst. The problem of abuse and mistreatment of women currently happening on a systemic level in the church today has not been adequately named or addressed out in the open.

I lament that we in the church have failed at offering sufficient support to those who are most in need of healing because the extent to which women are being harmed and in need of healing has largely been kept a secret.

CALL TO ACTION: SPEAK!

Yet why has this beautiful system of support remained secret and in the shadows? I believe that the church is so resistant to having its shadow side of abuse be known and out in the open that even those of us in positions of offering life-giving support to those who have been harmed must operate in secret, because naming that such abuse takes place would be "harming the church." But the church is the people. All women who have been harmed are the church! I am the church, too. To not address the rampant misogyny of our past and our present is to suggest that we are not the church. If naming this abuse "harms" church-as-business, then I look toward the good that comes from outing the injustice.

It's time that we rise up from the silence and speak aloud of the systemic oppression that women experience that happens in the name of God. It's time that men and women come out from the shadows to stand in solidarity with women who have been harmed at this time. It's time to name the injustices that we have seen and experienced. It's time to fully see the magnitude of this secret system as it rises up from an oppressive silence. It's time that the secret system of support comes out, in the open! It's time for those of us in this secret system to make connections, speak aloud, hold hands in this work, and organize for a better way. These women are our sisters, our mothers, our daughters, our neighbors, our pastors, and our friends. Cry out! Rise up! It's time for our justice! It's time. I lament that it's taken this long.

I lament that, today, liability is a dominating reason to control the narrative rather than faithful action in the name of Christ. Numbers (both membership numbers and financial numbers) are a motivating factor for the church's typical response to accusations of sexual harassment, harm, or wrongdoing, which is to force parties to sign a non-disclosure agreement (NDA).

I lament that NDAs are even an option in such situations. The desire to control the narrative and keep the wounded quiet only serves to fester the wound and increase the disease that is leading to atrophy of the church. We should all have the freedom to share our experiences and stories. Such honesty shines a light on injustice. This is how we learn and grow. It is healing for the person sharing their story and healing for others who hear their story and know they aren't alone. Shining a light on these situations is what will kill the systemic disease of harm. Transparency leads to honesty and integrity and encourages others to come forward. After all, there are many of us that have laments to dig up and turn over, tilling the soil for new seeds of life.

I lament that the reason I was told at the end of it all that I would be free to speak and not asked to sign an NDA is because I was so "faithful" throughout the process of the canonical trial. *Faithful* meaning that I denied myself the dignity of speaking up when I endured the repeated judgement and accusations from parishioners who were kept from knowing the full story when accusations were made about me. *Subservient* when I was not allowed on church property as though I did something wrong. *Faithful* when the bishop refused to simply define what happened as sexual harassment despite having written proof and multiple psychologists telling him otherwise. I lament that I was ridden with shame and in trauma, making me easy to further suppress in order to be considered faithful and "a priest in good standing."

I lament the vast number of people who have been harmed by the church that have suffered in silence. Many victims in a hierarchical, patriarchal church are still under NDAs (also called "gag orders") and are unable to speak or don't know the specifics of what is allowed. If you can, speak from a place of solidarity and support. I lament that, for years, lingering shame has kept me quiet even when I was allowed to speak. It's time that those of us who can speak up do so together.

This is what I know to be true: there *will* be a church in the future that is Christ's Church. It may look very different than what we've got now. In order for institutional churches to step into the future—to step into the spiritual advancement that we are called to, it is critical in this moment that we take a look at our shadow selves and that we look transparently at how we can treat one another better. We cannot take this system of harming women in the church with us into the future.

> There cannot be a future church where women are being harmed. This system of advancing men who are harming women still continues and it must stop.

I care tremendously about the future of the church and I hope that the denomination that I love and came from, in addition to other denominations and churches, will be a part of this change. In order to be a part of this change, we have to meet thiso moment with a spirit of honesty and integrity. We have to shine a light on our shadow side.

Seeds of Hope: The Compost Pile Grows
with the Lament of Others

Here, take a shovel. Put on your gardening gloves. Raise your voice with mine. Let us tell our stories while we dig deep together. After all, there cannot be new growth from seeds without first making compost. It begins with sharing our stories and adding our sorrows to the compost pile, each one a seed. We plunge deep down, into soil that has become hardened through neglect. We dig deep and turn it up and over, watering it with our tears, our cries, and our collective lament. We add our anger, our broken dreams, and our hopes. We summon our ancestors of the faith and the ancestors in our families. We call on the bones of discarded victims to rise up and gather around. God knows their stories—some have been shared, and some were kept silent until their deaths. We need all of our community, across the generations. We add our stories and feelings, neglected and discarded like old peels and rinds. The sun shines on our glistening faces as we dig deep, but we are in this work together. We linger there, leaning on the handle of our shovels, looking at our growing pile of compost, acknowledging that we were never alone in this, although it felt that way. It feels good to do this hard work together.

Here is the plain truth: the key to a beautiful, authentic future church[25] that is faithful to the life of Jesus Christ and full of integrity begins with the compost of our collective stories of pain, shame, and lament. The more putrid the compost is, the better it will be to fertilize a new way, born from humility and brokenness. This is the Jesus way. It's the way of nature and of life itself. Through death, new life will emerge. Through sorrow, joy will peek through these gray, dismal days like a brilliant light. It is the story of resurrection. After we mourn the death of what was, the power of new life, as shown to us in every tree and perennial flower, will be more beautiful than any of us can ever ask or imagine.

Will you join me? There is a pile of extra shovels and plenty of dirt to dig up and turn over. Share your story with those of us who are considered the "lost sheep." Once we share our stories we can find each other. We are not alone. Let our tears water and fertilize the compost pile and give it to God. Let God birth new life from it in God's time.

An Unsolicited, Yet Sincere Gift

I have been doing the work of digging up the hardened soil of my past. I have explored the shadows of pain and harm. I dig them up and offer my humiliating stories, my wounds, and my shortfalls, so that you may see just one small example of smelly compost that became fertile ground for a new way in me. I do not offer my story in order to harm the church in any way whatsoever. I do not harbor resentment, ill will, and certainly not revenge. I have forgiven those who hurt or harmed me, intentionally or not. Even though, to this day, I stand on the margins, with much of my time outside of the church, I have great love and immense hope for the gathered body of followers of Jesus. I have great love, respect, and admiration for countless parishioners, clergy, and yes, bishops too. I raise my hands cupped together, full of this soil for you to peer into and explore, in hopes that it will urge the church on its journey to participate in the very story of Jesus it seeks to proclaim—a resurrection of a new way. I urge the church toward naming the harm happening to women and others in the shadows. I offer this fertile compost as proof that God will turn the most rotten past into a beautiful foundation for our future. May the church show that it believes in resurrection by walking through the shadows of death and pain. May it stop quieting victims with NDAs and "rules" that benefit institutions over people. May the church stop using lawsuits to protect their financial assets over the lives of the wounded. May they proclaim the story of Jesus by embodying it! By becoming it!

I know this journey through the shadows—digging down to the roots in me—is a gift because it was the sorrow and trauma that I endured in the church that created a putrid compost pile for God to sow the seeds of a new life in Christ in me.

In this compost, with the gift of time and healing, and with the gift of grace and Christ eyes, three specific seeds began to sprout: the seeds of Christ consciousness, God's Rhema, and the Divine Feminine. [26]

It is a testament to God's goodness that even in the darkest hour of my life, God was moving in me and through me in ways I could have never imagined at the height of my sorrow. This is the gift that awaits the church when we combine our stories of sorrow. God will do a new thing! Resurrection is our story. I stand here on the margins, my hand outstretched to yours, offering you accompaniment on this challenging journey, for I have already walked this way before. I'm here to tell you that God will raise up a new creation.

A not-so-quiet revolution is on her way. With every seed of lament that we sow, I pray that reform and a new way will rise up. I pray that God will soften the hardened soil in order to give life to the seeds of our lament.

But first we have to honor what is dead and give it to God.

I WILL NOT WALK AWAY FROM JESUS

I may have evolving views of organized religion, a heart full of lament, and scars from his followers, but I have hope in resurrection, and I will not walk away from Jesus.

I will not walk away from Jesus, who surrounded me with gentle comfort in my pain while the church I served didn't allow me on their property when I reported an ugly truth.

I will not walk away from Jesus, who was my strength and my encourager in speaking truth to power when I stood up for myself to the bishop.

I will not walk away from Jesus, who guided my path toward healing and wholeness, who moved through mental health providers, and who shepherded me as I got back on my feet.

I will not walk away from Jesus, who was with my husband and my family during this time of trauma and hardship.

I will not walk away from Jesus, who inspires the countless good-hearted, kind, just Christians who bring hope to one another, their communities, and me.

I will not walk away from Jesus, who continues to inspire and move through so many people who no longer feel at home in church as we know it today.

I will not walk away from Jesus, who again and again comes to me even as I am on the margins of church, through church leaders: clergy, parishioners, friends, and colleagues who long to be part of the church in new ways, and who take my hand so we can do this together.

I understand why many walk away from the church. I have experienced the judgement, the gossip, and the prioritizing of money over concern for the downtrodden that has caused so many to walk away from Christianity. But the aspect of American Christianity that acts like a soul-less business is not Jesus. I will not walk away from Jesus. In fact, because of the risen Christ, I too have been born anew. I have experienced new life. I have been released from the shame that that so many church people attempted to put on me. I have experienced the liberating love of Christ outside of the church.

I will not walk away from Jesus, my North Star. That hardship may have weakened me. But through the shattering of the ego and the shattering of my one-dimensional view of church, the light of God shone brightly through the cracks.

I will not walk away from Jesus. In the telling of my story, I send the remaining vestiges of shame to the compost pile. Shame no longer takes up energy in me. That traumatic experience no longer defines me. The patterns of patriarchy, control, fear, covered-up truths, fear of liability, trauma response, rejection, and lack of compassion—the shadow patterns of a hierarchical, patriarchal church do not have a hold on me, do not define me, and will no longer silence me. I have come to a place of deep compassion for my past self, who did the best I could at that time. And actually, I have come to a place of compassion for the church I love that is now in decline. I look back on my story and see a majority of good people who were part of a broken system they sought to protect. I have compassion for the millions of victims of the church over the centuries. We are all beloved children of God. Worthy of compassion, yes. And worthy of a more noble expression of *church*—the community that follows Christ—than what we've got now.

That hardship may have weakened me. It may have brought me to my knees in pain and sorrow, but through my weakness, through the shattering of the ego, the shattering of my one-dimensional view of church, through the shattering of all that was, the light of God shone brightly through the cracks. The light of God cannot be extinguished!

I pull back the curtains on my story in hopes that it will aid in shining a light on a dark part of Christianity today. It's time to turn a corner. It's time to walk out on faith, taking steps toward what is next, toward what is a more compassionate and loving expression of faith, free from the grip of empire, free from the grip of fear, money, and control. Not only will I not walk away from Jesus, I will follow him as he liberates us beyond church walls.

Chapter 4
Reflection Questions

- What are some laments that you have about the church?
- How have you participated in or benefitted from the very aspects of church that you lament?
- In what ways have you minimized your own self to fit the "cookie-cutter" stereotypes of what Christians should be like?
- What is it like for you to linger in the shadow side of church?
- How does a church-as-business, membership-oriented model of church limit our ability to follow Jesus? Who does it leave out?
- Do you have a story of pain, shame, or lament to add for our collective compost pile? Who can support you if you choose to share it with others?
- What are some seeds of hope you see in your community, local church, or gatherings of people you care about?

PART TWO: THRIVE

A New Understanding—The Eternal Present

5

Christ Consciousness: Resurrection of a New Understanding

> *"No problem can be solved with the same level of consciousness that created it."*
> —ALBERT EINSTEIN

After the harassment, the threats, the cover up, and the shunning, it was like a lightning bolt struck hard in my life. It shattered the way I saw church. Church-as-empire shattered, and the truth was illuminated for me. My time of suffering felt dark and isolating. I was brought down low. My ego was shattered, my role as a priest felt shattered, and there was nothing left but the essence of Christ light within me, low but steadily burning. In the dark night of my soul, I realized that the essence of me was more than any role. The essence of me did not need church-as-business in order to shine my Christ light. In the absence of ego, fully surrendered, the essence of me was so connected to God that, with time, my intuition showed me truths that eluded my prior naïveté, as well as my cognitive mind. The illusion of the church-as-empire needed to be shattered in order for me to awaken to the truth that the mystic Christ is everywhere and does not belong only to the institutional church. Perhaps it is advantageous for the institutional church to hide the truths of the mystic Christ. The very concept of the mystic Christ signifies that a person can have a direct experience of the living Christ without any intermediary. Not only can Christ be directly experienced, but this direct encounter can happen anywhere, including outside of church. The mystic Christ is not commonly known or talked about, yet can be experienced anywhere by anyone, at any time, which means that I saw anew! The very root of me experienced a rebirth—I literally felt born again, with new eyes, and a new understanding of the world. Now, I could see that the mystic Christ was within me and around me all along. The mystic Christ is also in you.

GOD WITHIN

> *"Abide in me as I abide in you."*
> —JESUS IN THE GOSPEL OF JOHN 15:4

Despite the stereotypical Christian concept of God, the Bible describes God as within and all around us. This is a strange revelation to most of us who were raised in the Christian faith because the awareness that Christ abides within us was not reflected in most of our Sunday School teachings. The truth that God is within me and within you is often not emphasized in present-day Christian culture. How many Sunday School classes have you attended, how many sermons have you heard, and how many conversations have you had in the church that have helped to strengthen your understanding that Christ abides within us?

Chances are, if you were raised in a family of faith, you were taught primarily that God was outside of yourself. For many people who were raised as Christian in the United States and throughout the world, God has been presented on coloring pages and in books as an older, white, male deity with white hair and an authoritative presence. God is often presented as being physically far away, such as in heaven. Many people were taught to fear God and believed they were far away from God, even as they heard that God is Love. The culture of church often emphasizes dichotomies and separation between God and the individual, squarely placing "the church" as the sole intermediary between Jesus Christ and millions of his followers by using authority, power, control, shame, and fear. Unfortunately, some aspects of Christian culture today cause trauma and pain by teaching people to fear an eternity in hell if they sin in any way without asking for forgiveness. They emphasize Bible verses that cause fear while downplaying loving and universal concepts. Distorted teachings meant to cast fear and judgement have understandably pushed people away from faith communities and soured our concept of church.

A Hidden and Revolutionary Concept

Christian culture, as we have come to know it thus far, has not emphasized the concept that Christ abides in us because this could threaten the authority of church leaders in our current model of church. If followers of Jesus felt confident that Christ abided in them and if they knew how to pray and live their lives with that amazing truth, it would change everything. It's the difference between walking up a hill with much effort and soaring in the air, carried effortlessly by wind. The concept that Christ abides in each of us is revolutionary.

Why? Because we are no longer passive to events in our lives when we learn to recognize and recover the Divinity within us. When we begin to recognize and recover the truth that Christ abides within us, then we can turn within, to the still small voice of God, to listen to what wisdom emerges from the quiet. When we come to an awareness that God is within us, it changes how we view ourselves.

Can you imagine that the divinity within you is just as beautiful, majestic, illuminating, and glorious as any altar, any church, or any cathedral? There is divinity within *you*!

When we live our lives understanding that our body is our sanctuary, then we treat our bodies better. When we understand that the spark of divinity is truly within us, then the notion of honoring our need for rest and time for renewal becomes foundational to taking care of ourselves and our spark of divinity within.

And when we understand that God is within us, then we begin to realize that God is within others too. We can imagine how the realization that God is everywhere, abiding in each of us shifts our consciousness and our actions. When we see everyone as having a spark of divinity within them, then we see their inherent worth. Recognizing divinity in others allows us to have a deeper compassion for others. When the revolutionary concept that each and every one of us has Christ/God within us begins to settle inside of us, then we can begin to conceive of our interconnectedness and explore the potentials and possibilities that emerge.

Christ Consciousness

> "In the beginning was the Word, and the Word was with God, and the Word was God. He was in the beginning with God. All things came into being through him, and without him not one thing came into being. What has come into being in him was life, and the life was the light of the people."
>
> —JOHN 1:1–4

The Gospel of John doesn't begin with the physical birth of Jesus in a manger. The Gospel of John acknowledges that the Word made flesh (Jesus) has existed with God since the beginning of creation. This is the mystic Christ, who is everywhere, at all times. All things came into being through him! That includes you and me. All of creation, all people, all animals, the entire earth—we all came into being through the mystic Christ. And Wisdom, the Divine Feminine, was also there, as a "master worker," co-creating everything into existence.[27] Christ consciousness begins with the concept that Christ is within you, within me, within every person, and within the natural world.

The Ongoing Incarnation of Christ

After nearly two decades of leading Christmas Eve services, I was no longer serving as a parish priest since I was now working with churches around the country supporting their community engagement. I was invited to a local church to attend their Christmas Eve service and went with my family. It was everything I could have hoped for. The church members were warm and friendly to one another and my family. The singing was beautiful; you could feel the sincerity. The pastor, who clearly loved Jesus, preached a fine sermon. I looked around and it was a beautiful sight: church members in their holiday outfits, glowing candles, beautiful Scripture, music, evergreens and poinsettias. And yet, it didn't evoke the same feelings that Christmas Eve used to for me. I looked around and saw an elderly gentleman tapping the pew to the beat of the music. Everyone was glad to be there, and to be clear, I was too. There was nothing to complain about. It was a genuinely lovely Christmas Eve service. I sat with the curiosity that Christmas Eve services were no longer full of nostalgia for me, even though I had a very real and present connection with Jesus Christ in my life. I came to the conclusion that there were two reasons for this. First, experiencing how I was treated and how I saw the church operate behind the scenes effectively dampened my feelings of nostalgia associated with Christmas Eve and other services. But even more importantly, the concept of John 1:1–4 had taken over my understanding of the incarnation; it wasn't limited to Jesus being born as a baby. Christ consciousness allows me to experience the Word that has been there since the beginning of time in the thick of a forest with birds around me. I have experienced the Word, the Christ, in everyday activities with my children, on my sofa when I pray, when I cook and eat with loved ones, when I serve at a food pantry, even when I work. To be able to be fully conscious with the awareness that all things and people around me came into being through the Word means that my day-to-day life feels sacred and full of God. I have learned to see incarnation everywhere. To be clear, this doesn't mean that church is less sacred; it means that our lives and the world outside of the church can be experienced as more sacred. Our eyes and hearts can be open to our day-to-day lives being full of people and experiences that include the living Christ. This is Christ consciousness. While the nostalgia of a special Christmas Eve service has faded for me now, the holiness of that day remains incredibly special to me. Moreover, the unique and sacred potential of each and every day, each moment, and every person I encounter is sacred. The holy is truly everywhere. Every day can be an encounter with the divine, not just Sundays or special occasions.

Seeing our lives and the world through the lens of John 1:1–4 invites us to a much wider understanding of God. This is Christ consciousness. I have found that the easiest way to experience Christ consciousness is to stay fully present to the sacredness and everyday-ness of life right in front of you and to experience Christ-in-all-things in your life. Rather than having certain times in our lives to experience the sacred, such as going to church or praying before a meal, Christ consciousness invites us to see Christ in all people and in all places, all the time. Both of these concepts can coexist. I regularly pray and set time apart for God even as I seek to see Christ in all people, in all places, all the time.

Practicing Christ consciousness includes honoring the inner Wisdom in us, She who is and has been present throughout creation.[28] This integration happens over time, with a spirit of mindfulness and observation, which serves to calm and slow down the overactive mind. With practice, mindfulness and observation bring a spirit of patience, wisdom, and intuition. Practicing mindfulness as a means to Christ consciousness allows us to trust our feelings. We have all experienced times when our feelings can get out of control and go to extremes. Practicing mindfulness acknowledges the power of your mind, your thoughts, and your feelings. It begins with a deep awareness of your thoughts and feelings. Observation of our feelings and reactions allows us to notice the times when we need to proactively balance our perspective. We can do this by allowing a better thought or a healthier response to something. We do not need to be victims of our thoughts and feelings. We can co-create a more balanced and healthy frame of mind. When both the thinking mind and the feelings we have are in a state of balance and not out of control, then we are able to welcome intuition. By practicing mindfulness, we cultivate a heightened awareness, and then, our feelings can become very trustworthy. In a balanced state of mind, if I feel positive and good when I am around someone new, then I can trust my feelings that this person is good for me. If I read or hear something and I notice a sense of anxiety or concern, then I may have reason to be wary.

We have been taught to doubt our feelings, but in fact, they can be a superpower for us; like a sixth sense that gives us information ahead of the rational mind.

The mystic Christ that is in all things is also a part of our beautiful minds, hearts, and feelings. We have been taught to be doubting or cautious of our feelings but, in actuality, our feelings can be a great strength.

Christ consciousness grows and develops when we allow for gaps and spaces in our days and when we give ourselves the gift of staying in the present moment to notice what God is doing in us and through us. I can make a puzzle with my daughter, watch my sons play either basketball or their sax, and cook dinner for my family, and I can do these things in a state of hurriedness and impatience, jumping every time I get a text, mindlessly looking at my phone all the time, or I can do so with a spirit of Christ consciousness, which allows me to admire my daughter's determination and silliness, notice the passion my boys have for their chosen hobbies, and cook dinner with a spirit of love. Experiencing Christ consciousness does not always require an upheaval of our daily lives. I have found that by saying "no" to some things I didn't really want to do anyway, I can say "yes" to a more balanced rhythm of life. Just a little more space in my days without running from one thing to the next and less screen time allows me to experience a state of ongoing communing with God. In some ways, I have an ongoing dialogue with God and many other times I am simply aware of the presence of divinity around me at all times. The sacredness of the everyday is full of the presence of God when we are conscious of it.

A Spiral of Expanding Awareness

Christ consciousness is a spiral that seeks to reclaim more than a limited, reactive, cognitive understanding of reality. It is a deep awareness that involves our senses, our heart, our mind, and our soul. It is holistic, meaning that Christ consciousness seeks to reclaim a whole, unfragmented sense of reality, and the pursuit of this understanding is, by its nature, healthy and good. I am fully present to observe what Spirit is doing in the world, around us, and within me. I am aware of my mind, my emotions, my intuition, and what is happening around me, all at once. I start with observing my interior world of thoughts and feelings, and my awareness spirals out to deeply observe people and the world around me.

When we are in a posture of quickly reacting to something, we forgo a more holistic response. Christ consciousness is the return to a deeper awareness, a deeper observation, and a more patient posture that allows us to experience the mystic Christ in ourselves, in our loved ones, in our community, and in nature. I don't feel concerned about where I will end up because I am inspired by God's love, not fear. I am also deeply aware that Christ is everywhere around me now. There is nothing about Love that I need to fear. When I live into this awareness, then I sense that the sacred is everywhere. There is nowhere God is not. In Christ consciousness, I am present in the here and now, which means that anxiety about the future and depression about the past loses its grip and power over me.

It was this tiny flame of divinity within me that could not be extinguished when I was at my lowest, that continued to burn, eventually healing my shattered heart. This spark is at the root of us, within each of us. Allowing that light—that energy of Love—to grow in me, and increasing my awareness of it within me, within others, and in the world around us has, without a doubt, changed my life.

Spiral Fractal of Spiritual Expansion
(Jesus' Spiral Fractal Prayer)

Jesus is beloved worldwide because he lived a life that embodied interconnectedness with all whom he encountered. His deep compassion, teachings, and life events are respected, revered, and compelling to people of many faiths around the world. His most extensive prayer takes up the entirety of Chapter 17 in the Gospel of John and reveals his all-encompassing heart of compassion. If you are able, follow along with John Chapter 17 on your phone or in your Bible. Jesus prays in a spiral fractal that expands outward. He begins by praying for himself and prays that he remains connected with God the Father: "glorify your Son so that the Son may glorify you." He even acknowledges that he has been present with God since "before the world existed"(verse 5).

Next, he prays for those who are closest to him when he prays for "those whom you gave me from the world." He is praying for his community around him, the ones who believe in him and follow him. In verse 12, he even says, "I guarded them, and not one of them was lost except the one destined to be lost." Notice how important his followers are to him. Jesus places a priority on those who aren't lost. You are not lost to him if you choose to believe or follow him, even if you aren't an official part of organized religion today.

He also makes his purpose known in verse 13: "I speak these things in the world so that they may have my joy made complete in themselves." He wants us to know joy! He believes that his joy completes and fulfills us. He wants anyone affiliated with him to experience his *joy*. He then stands in solidarity with those who feel hated in this world since he also has been hated in this world. He sees you when you feel hated by others. He understands you. And he prays for God's protection over you.

And then his prayer spirals outward again. Next, in verse 20, he prays "on behalf of those who *will* believe in me through their word, that they may all be one." While he is alive, he prays for those who will believe in him in the future. In the same way he was with God from the beginning of creation, he is with us now, into the future. And he prays for our unity—from the past to the present and all around the world: may we all be One. He also acknowledges in verses 21–23 that God is in him and Jesus is in God and prays that we may be in them. Jesus says, "I in them and you in me, that they may be one." This is our mystic Christ, praying for generations of people around the world that haven't yet been born. Acknowledging that he is in us, and we are in God. We are fully connected *already*.

There is one more layer to this beautiful prayer of Jesus. After he prays for all believers, from the past to the future, he prays for the world. In verse 23 he says, "so that the world may know that you have sent me and have loved them even as you have loved me." He wants the *entire world* to know that God loves them. He came for the whole world to know God's love! He closes this spiral prayer asking that "the love with which you have loved me may be in them, and I in them."

This stunningly beautiful prayer and its ramifications have stayed with me for years. And I hope that you too will let it soak into your soul, particularly when you feel parched and worn from life's difficulties. He starts by praying for himself, then his community and followers closest to him, and then he prays for all of us in the future who will believe in him. He prays for our unity and acknowledges that we are always within Jesus and God and that they are within us. And then he prays for the whole world, that we may all know the love of God. No one is left out. After all, we all "came into being through him."[29]

SELF

COMMUNITY

WORLD

When he prayed that prayer, it included *us* because he prayed for us, in the future. He prayed intending to include *you*, reading these words right now. This prayer reminds me that 1) it is not wrong to pray for yourself and care for yourself first, because Jesus did that, and 2) prayers and spiritual understandings are meant to spiral outward and expand. This is not a linear prayer. This prayer reverberates throughout all of history, from the beginning of creation to a future we cannot yet see or know. This is a spiral fractal prayer because it is ongoing. He has prayed a prayer that you and I, and everyone in the world, know that Jesus and God are within our hearts, and we are within them. Our divinity lies within us. And yet, although Scripture makes it plain, it is the biggest secret about our faith because the patriarchal (outward) representation of Christianity as we currently know it, which depends on religious leaders acting as mediators, has mostly kept it from us. Until now.

The spiral fractal isn't just about Jesus' prayer in John 17; it's about the unique, ongoing way that he shared love with the world that also spirals outward. The very act of Jesus sharing his message with fishermen, women, and castoffs, who then shared his message with their loved ones and neighbors, who shared it over generations and generations is also a spiral fractal. The growth of our faith was a spiral of sharing in a spirit of expansion. Across countries and continents, across languages and through families, through books, stories, and compassionate action, the love of God has been shared.

SPIRALS VERSUS PYRAMIDS

And yet, an honest account must also acknowledge the many ways that violence and force has accompanied the spread of our faith, even today. True discipleship includes sharing the love of God in our hearts and sharing how the teachings of Christ have impacted us, without coercion or force, but simply from a pure spirit of Love. Jesus' spiral fractal of expansion spreads Love, even expanding outward into the cosmos. The nature of hierarchical church, however, is not known for its love that spirals outward in community. Rather, power, authority, and resources primarily go up, to the top.

In this stage of development in Christianity, we got it wrong when we combined coercion and force with sharing the Love of God found in Christ. Good News is not so good when combined with violence; disregarding cultures; instilling fear, shame and control; executing or harming women; or enslaving people of color. Perhaps, as part of our healing, we need to pray for the past, the present, and the future like Jesus did in John 17, with the same pure heart that Jesus had. Jesus moved mountains with love, not harm.

The majority of Christian churches function in the shape of a pyramid, even though that is not the pattern or teaching of Jesus. Even if a church is not a part of a hierarchical denomination, chances are, the church functions in the shape of a pyramid with a minimum of three levels: congregants, committees and boards, and staff and/or clergy at the top. In this church model, the minister or pastor has spiritual authority and is often expected to preach sermons that educate, inspire, inform faith, and prompt congregants to give, supporting the financial security of the church. If a church has a property need or a programmatic need, that will often be prioritized above helping meet financial needs of those in the community. Staffing needs, too, often come before giving to those in need. Most church ministries are defined by what is taking place inside the church building, rather than the impact the body of Christ is having among the community around them. The whole concept of church and the ministries of the church have been too tied to church buildings and property. They have become too tied to the programmatic needs of paying congregants while significantly less time, energy, and resources are allocated to the community in need. Meanwhile, Jesus encountered people primarily outside the synagogue and the Temple—along streets, by a well, at dinner tables, in the community, while traveling, while washing feet, eating, and healing. He constantly sought out opportunities to embody the love of God in the world around him regardless of whether it was a Sabbath day or not, and regardless of whether he was in the synagogue or not. In fact, most of his teachings and compassionate action took place outside of the synagogue, among the people. Conversely, even though churches are tied to our buildings, we all know of church buildings that are busy on Sundays but mostly sit empty during the week, potential assets to the community that go unused.

In hierarchical denominations, each church also gives money to regional and national levels of church structure to support the bishops, superintendents, staff, and their denominations' offices. Financial support continues to flow up to support presiding bishops and national leaders, their staff, and programs. Indeed, much of this funding supports worthy causes. However, the size and strength of hierarchical churches can, unfortunately, lead to an emphasis on financial gain for the purpose of supporting the hierarchical church over the purpose of all of God's people increasing the reign of Love in the communities around us. As leaders gain authority and power further up the hierarchical ranks, they are bestowed special titles and honorifics, and they are expected to uphold the traditions of the denomination they lead. As leaders rise, their leadership is often focused more and more on supporting the denomination and less on the communities around the congregations that affiliate with the denomination. It is always inspiring to me when church leaders are consistent in putting resources and energy into local communities in the name of Christ. This is so basic to Jesus' teachings, yet often does not happen.

In the shape of a pyramid, authority, power, and the vast majority of finances go up, staying within the hierarchical organization that is the church, rather than going out into the community. Most people giving to the church do not question this pattern, despite the fact that it does not model what Jesus valued. "My kingdom is not of this world," Jesus said.[30] We must fully acknowledge, even linger on, the reality of where we are now, with finances and resources being controlled in an upward and inward direction, before we can begin to imagine what church could look like.

Freedom to Expand

The opposite of the energy of the church (resources and finances) being controlled to go upward and inward is the freedom to expand outward. A key part of the spiral fractal is that it starts with the individual in their spirit, rooted to God—rooted to pure Love. Consider the most inward part of a flower, connected to its stem, which is connected to its roots.

The flower inherently has everything it needs to grow and become all that it can be. It's all contained in a tiny seed. It simply needs water and light, and it innately knows how to grow, expand, bloom, and even create more flowers. It is free to blossom and grow! This is a natural part of not only the plant kingdom but all of creation. If creation is free, and light is abundant, and co-creation is natural and easily provided for by the patterns of nature, shouldn't it be *even more so* for humanity? Yet, our history of sharing the love of God, at least in the Christian tradition, still carries the seeds of control, shame, violence, harm, and a lack of transparency.

We have some weeding and pruning to do to return to our innate desire to experience the freedom and openness to grow, expand, and experience love and joy. On a macro level, many of us first need the freedom to grieve what we need to grieve. We each need the freedom to experience joy in a way that allows our spirits to thrive. And we need to be free to use our specific talents and gifts. We all need that freedom. We need to honor how God is moving in other people's hearts too. There is no one-size-fits-all. Organized religion cannot and should not work for everyone. True freedom in Christ is rooted in love that is available to us all. The spiral fractal that Jesus models inherently honors the freedom to experience how each of us is rooted to God, self, community, and cosmos. And yet it begins with the seed of truth that God abides within each of us.

A massive cultural shift is underway, which is the shift to understand that God, or Divine Love, is within us. All major religions describe God as Love, so I often use the term Divine Love to refer to God. The culture of patriarchy has furthered the notion that God is outside of ourselves. The culture of patriarchy uses hierarchy and outside authority (meaning, authority that is not you) to control the narrative about God and how we should live our lives. This era of patriarchy is slowly beginning to crack and break open. And since the industries that humanity has created have all come into existence under the realm of our patriarchal construct, we are experiencing vast upheavals. We see the remnants of many institutions crumbling and, indeed, current events and times of chaos indicate that they are putting up a nasty fight. Nearly every time we read or listen to the news or engage social media, we hear about corrupt politicians, war, a lack of compassion in our society, an epidemic of gun violence, exposures of harm being caused by celebrities and church leaders, and vitriol and judgement that spews across social media. Industries from health care, insurance, and government to education, church, and media are being exposed for seeking profit at the expense of their original purpose. As a result, there is an all-encompassing feeling of stress and insecurity among us all. We wonder, "Who can we trust, really? How can we protect ourselves? What about me matters to society? What are our values? Where is there love?" These industries further fuel our fear and our reaction. They create products to fix us, further fueling our insecurity as we rely more and more on things outside of ourselves. This cycle of patriarchal industry fueling our insecurity and fear is the inverse of the spiral fractal of love. *Watch this movie to take your mind off of life! Buy these guns to protect you and your family. Stock food, just in case. Only watch our news channel, not the others. The other political party is evil. Go to our church, not theirs. We are the ones that care for justice. Buy our product because we support this cause, which will help you. Wear these clothes. Alter this about your appearance.* On and on this steady drumbeat seeks to make us feel off-balance, promising us that whatever it is they are selling is the answer, at least until we try it and feel no better. This steady drumbeat fuels a narcissistic, insecure, fearful, and profit-driven society—the very opposite of Jesus' spiral fractal of Love. Our fear only feeds these patriarchal constructs that are crumbling, and the remaining vestiges that are starting to crumble are getting louder and louder. Collectively, we feel the instability. We feel the unease.

The Rise of the Divine Feminine: Expanding Our Concept of Divine Love

> "Does not wisdom call, and does not understanding raise her voice?. . .The Lord created me at the beginning of his work, the first of his acts long ago. . . .When he established the heavens, I was there. . . then I was beside him, like a master worker."
> —PROVERBS 8

Meanwhile, slowly and quietly, the Divine Feminine is rising. She has been there all along, known as Wisdom or Sophia in Holy Scripture. Now, before your stereotypes take over about what the "Divine Feminine" means, consider this: the Divine Feminine aspects of God have been under-represented in much of history as we have known it. We have leaned so much into the image of God as Father that our current expression of church has not incorporated the images of a God who comforts us as a mother comforts children (Isaiah 66:13), or who comforts us as a mother eagle hovering over her young (Deuteronomy 32:11), or God as a midwife caring for the baby just delivered (Psalms 22:9–10 and 71:6), or Jesus as a mother hen who gather chicks under her wings (Luke 13:34) or a housekeeper looking for a lost coin (Luke 15:8). We have known power and authority outside of ourselves in the realm of religion, societal institutions, and government. Divine Feminine values acknowledge the co-existence of an inner wisdom—an inner authority and divinity—and a deep interconnection with the earth. Millions of people are making decisions based on their inner authority about their food choices and their health, what news they consume and how much, and how they will show up in the world amidst these turbulent times.

And millions of people have already left institutional Christianity, while simultaneously venturing into the woods, listening to the wisdom from within, practicing yoga and meditation, experiencing sound baths, going on retreats, and cultivating Love in ways that feel supportive and healthy to them. Thousands of people are actively deconstructing the faith they were raised with, meaning that they are trusting themselves to reject the parts that were harmful to them, while considering what good may have been left out. The shift toward recognizing our sense of internal authority, and our divinity within, has already begun. The Divine Feminine is rising as a balance to centuries of patriarchy, of fitting in and conforming while minimizing who we are and what feels right for us. Rather than seeing God (the energy of Divine Love) as outside of ourselves and removed from us, we can experience God within us and all around us, as we are conscious that Divine Love is everywhere.

This energy of Divine Love that is both within us and all around us keeps us energetically intertwined with the ones we love. I am connected to my family even when we are apart. I am connected to my friends even when I don't see them regularly. That energy of love is God! It is the same divine energy that encompasses every part of our beautiful planet. This energy of love keeps all of creation humming, living, and alive. When I am conscious of this energy of love (God) that is all around us, then I am practicing Christ consciousness.

After my experience of harm in the church, I felt called to start a church in the south side of town. I wanted to be a priest to people who knew suffering and hardship and didn't hide from it. I wanted to be a priest on the other side of town because, like many of them, I needed God to get through life. After over a decade of spending the vast majority of my time as an ordained minister serving primarily within church walls, I began spending days at a time outside of the church. For a few years, I met neighbors in Section 8 Housing, I got to know the cashiers at *tiendas*, and I lingered in mobile home neighborhoods. I led a weekly Bible study in a homeless shelter where they gave me office space in a neglected room to be a pastoral presence to those staying there. I would comfort women who became sex workers, make crafts with children staying at the homeless shelter, play kickball with the kids in the neighborhood where our church would be, and show up to neighborhood meetings. Being with these people healed my wounded heart. We became church (the two or three gathered) in the humblest of ways. I felt like a caged bird that was set free. My whole image of what serving God looked like expanded so large it shattered my worldview. I had been trained to see serving God as serving inside the church, but once I began spending so much time in the community, it became apparent that the Spirit was moving just fine amongst people outside the church! My faith was saved, through them.

To start a new faith community, I began by listening for how the Spirit was already moving in the lives of the people. Listening to the Spirit is an ability we can cultivate. The more we practice it, the better we can perceive. I could listen and notice the ways that God was moving in their hearts, in their hopes and longings, and in their lives. When I pointed to it, they would affirm what I noticed. One neighbor was passionate about music and began teaching lessons to neighborhood children. He smiled broadly when I told him it seems like God was using his passion for music to bless the kids of the neighborhood. Once I started getting to know the community, it wasn't hard to pull together, or organize, our collective hopes for how we could be a blessing to the community. Most people want to be a blessing to others and their community. Most people want to be a part of the good happening where they live. Combining our hopes to be agents for good isn't hard, but it takes time and a sincere desire to listen. It takes slowing down and being attentive to the energy of Love that runs through us all. It reminds me of my abuelita, who taught me about Christ eyes. We need Christ eyes for the world around us. We can develop our Christ eyes to perceive the spark of divinity in ourselves and in others, and then combine our sparks of divinity so that we ignite the light of Christ in the world! In our little corner of town, we started a large, bustling bilingual food pantry, with leaders from the community and area churches. That's what the collective voices said we needed, and neighbors in our community helped to make it happen. We gathered the collective hopes and resources of two denominations on the national and local levels and gathered the goodwill of several area churches and organizations who all helped to create a church that is thriving and continuing to grow, to this day. You see, the energy of Love is inherently meant to grow and expand. The energy of Love doesn't want to be contained within four walls! But as my abuelita said, "This will change you." Seeing yourself, others, and the world through the lens of Christ consciousness will change the way you see the church and the world, and it's hard to go back. The Spirit wants to expand our concept of God. It longs to see divine love everywhere because that is our potential.

Our earth, full of living animals and plants, reverberates with this divine love. Our earth is conscious: our hopes, dreams, and fears are known because we are sentient beings whose feelings and emotions are transmitted through the energy of Divine Love. Thus far, at best our patriarchal, consumeristic society has been passive or unaware of this energy of divine love that runs through all of creation. At worst, we have been shielded from this eternal truth. Indigenous cultures that knew of the sacredness of all of creation were colonized and forced into new beliefs. But now, many of us are beginning to wake up to it; to become conscious of it. The Divine Feminine is rising.

This Changes Everything

Once we are conscious of this energy of love, we can choose how we use it. Like Jesus' spiral fractal prayer, I send this energy of love to myself.[31] I send it to my family and friends. I send this energy of love to those whom I encounter. I send this energy of love to those whose energy I entangle with, whether for work or for fun. I send this energy of love to war-torn areas of the world, to parts of our country that need it, and to humanity as a whole. This energy of love never runs out. It is limitless. Christ consciousness is the deep awareness that we are all connected in this way. I am aware of this divine love within me, and I am empowered to acknowledge, call, and direct the energy of love in me to be shared with others.

Several times now, a church leader has leaned into me quietly and said something like: "How do you do it?" Another said, "It seems like magic." "How do you grow faith communities when the church is in decline?" "How do you turn around the energy of a church in trouble?" "How do you balance your work with three children?" This is how—by consciously directing the energy of love in me and around me and encouraging others to do the same. This is the same energy of love that aids in co-creating my dreams and my prayers—the ones that will bring joy to me, my loved ones, and this world. In my prayers, in my silence, and in my goals, I am conscious that everything I do is rooted in love. Whether that is a Zoom call for my paid job, chopping vegetables and making dinner for my family, or going on a quiet walk, it's all rooted in the energy of love. When I work with churches, when I'm writing, and when I'm stopping my work at the end of the day, it is all rooted in love. When I'm reading a good book, that is rooted in love of self. There is a back and forth, an ebb and flow, an in and out of this energy of love. Love of self, love of others, love of the world. In and out, like breath. There is an art to balancing and moving with this energy of Love. This energy of divine love is unstoppable, unconditional, and insurmountable. It coexists in each and every one of us. Once we learn to use that energy and to develop that awareness, that's when it feels like magic happens. This, too, is Christ consciousness. This is what following Jesus can look like. It took a shattering of my faith to understand that God's love does not require or even prefer an institutional church to move through. Such a shattering is not a requirement for others. And yet, I do believe that Christ eyes that are open and aware of what is of God's pure love and what is not help us to see the potential of how God moves in our lives in broader ways.

Jesus was a master at using the divine energy of love to teach, to spread love when he told stories, to heal, to feed, to travel, and to spark a movement of followers. He utilized the energy of divine love to inspire and spread love to others. We still feel the reverberations of Christ's love today. Like his prayer in John 17, he prayed for the past and the future, and the impact is ongoing. In the same way, following Jesus does not start and end in a church building. It starts and ends with the sharing of love for the good of each other, our selves, and this world.

It can take some time to make this spiritual shift in how we see and understand the world around us. It is countercultural because there is nothing to purchase or obtain outside of yourself in order to increase your connection to God in this way. Christ consciousness does not require a church building or an altar because it can arise from anyone willing to lay aside ego and be open to God in the present moment. Whether you are in the woods, in your home, at work, on the subway, on a walk, washing dishes, in a hospital, mowing your yard, or caring for children, you have the ability to experience the world as though every person that you encounter is part of the mystic Christ. Each person and even the earth contains the spark of divinity—the energy of Love.

Christ consciousness is the awareness that Divine Love is within you and everyone you encounter. The Divine Love of God is also within the earth; indeed, all things that came to being came from God. Your awareness of the power of that is Christ consciousness. Your ability to perceive, listen, and communicate with Divine Love in the world allows you to hear your unique Divine rhema.

Reflection Questions: Chapter 5

- When were you first made aware of Christ abiding within you?
- Describe a time when you have experienced the sacredness of the everyday-ness of life.
- What are your thoughts about the revolutionary aspects of "Christ abides in you" (the way it impacts the compassion we have for ourselves and others, the way we care for ourselves and the earth, the way that we listen to God within)?
- How are you impacted by the notion that Jesus' prayer in John Chapter 17 includes you?
- Compare and contrast the spiral fractal shape of spreading our faith outward with the pyramid shape of power and authority going up.
- How have you observed or experienced patriarchal institutions crumbling around you and how do you resonate with the concept of the Divine Feminine rising?
- Have you experienced an increased desire to recognize your own internal authority? How does it feel to consider that as part of the collective Divine Feminine rising?
- How does the notion of Christ consciousness, the rising of the Divine Feminine, and Divine Love shift your understanding of God's movement in you and in the world?

6

Listening for God's Rhema (God's Word to You)

Cultivating Rhema with Times of Stillness and Solitude

Rhema is a spiritual revelation or communication that God is bringing to you personally, with no one and nothing in the middle. The concept of God speaking a specific word, known as rhema in Greek, is found 70 times in the New Testament. Rhema and logos both mean word, but logos refers to a universal word from God, and rhema is a personal word from God about your life. Rhema is best heard in times of stillness and/or solitude. In John 15:7, we read, "If you abide in me, and my words (rhema) abide in you, ask for whatever you wish, and it will be done for you."

In my time of deep suffering, I was driven to listen for a word from God to my aching heart. Over time, I learned how to hear God well and was inspired and comforted by what I was hearing. I am long past my stage of suffering now, but I have maintained my desire to listen to divine rhema as it enhances my faith and benefits me and others in many ways. We each need time alone to hear the still small voice of God, and each person is fully capable of discerning what that spirit is saying to them. The rhema

I have been receiving is to share with others and teach others how to hear rhema clearly in their lives. Again, anyone is capable of hearing rhema. You don't need a degree in theology or to be a member of a church. It requires nothing of you but a listening and willing heart and a little quiet time.

Intuition is a primary way we can listen to our divine rhema. Intuition is a deep knowing and understanding that comes in clearly when we quiet our mind and allow ourselves to be open to noticing signs and synchronicities around us, and open and listening to the still small voice within us that is rooted in Divine Love. It is not by accident that many of us have been taught to doubt our intuition by a patriarchal church that benefits when we doubt ourselves and place our spiritual authority in the hands of another. We each are able to cultivate our intuition, and many women, in particular, can attest to examples of when their intuition was helpful to them in providing comfort, safety, and assurance. If your intuition is rooted in love, then it is of God.

As much as we need community, we also need times of solitude and stillness. It is in solitude when I am conscious of being in community with God/Divine Love, Jesus, angels, ancestors, and the spiritual realm of support and guidance that I can experience in the quiet but cannot see. That communion of saints sustains me and allows me to bring the highest version of myself to community with others. Solitude, then, does not replace community. Rather, it enhances and advances community. We need both.

By stillness, I mean stillness of the mind. Stillness of internal thoughts. I can have stillness of the mind while on a walk. Repetitive movements like walking or gardening can calm the overactive mind. Stillness and solitude allow us to hear divine communication (rhema). When music is loud or there is a lot of chatting and conversation, or our lives are so busy we feel hectic and harried, it is harder to hear Spirit. When the television is on in the background or there is always noise, it can be harder to hear Spirit speak personally to you and through you.

Rediscovering Jesus as North Star

We are entering a time when world events seem chaotic. Upheavals, uncoverings, floodings, breaking news, war, turbulent changes, and emotional revelations can understandably leave us feeling on edge, anxious, sad, angry, fearful, and worn down. Yet the North Star remains unchanged. Stars, constellations, planets, and the moon are in constant movement, yet Polaris, the North Star, beams as a guiding light. For centuries the North Star has served as a guiding point for travelers on land and sea.

By listening to God's unique word to us, our rhema, we hear specific guidance for us. The spirit, teachings, life, and love of Jesus serve as the North Star for us during the shifts and changes of life. Jesus as North Star directs us toward transforming and transmuting the compost of anger, despair, and fear to forgiveness, peace, grounding, ease, and joy.

> Jesus has pointed me toward liberation and healing through forgiveness. Through the power of Christ, I have forgiven the church, the diocese, the wider institution, and the people of the church that harmed me.

I know that most of them are good people, but they are part of a system (the institutional church) that has perpetuated harm. Just by being Christians in the church, we become part of a system that has a history of harm, even if we don't have the big picture (the Christ eyes) of it happening. I forgive them all, including myself, and I know that God forgives us all. Not only have I forgiven them, some of my dearest friends are from the very church that hurt me. My journey of keeping my eye on

Christ has brought me back to a full circle of beautiful friendships and a peace in my heart that only Christ can give.

He guides us on a path from the sting of death to the joy of resurrection in our lives. His teachings are universal, his love expansive. Christianity will go through changes as it evolves to meet the needs of people, yet Jesus is our North Star. We will go through stages of pain, anger, hurt, forgiveness, renewal, and strength—yet Jesus is our North Star. Jesus, as North Star, is there for us when we are children learning basic stories, when we are teenagers exploring our values and freedoms, and as adults navigating the beautiful and difficult aspects of life. No matter whether we are on the margins of church, on the outside of community, part of any religion at all, no matter our age, our ethnicity, our language, no matter who we love or what secrets we carry, Jesus can be our North Star, guiding us toward the direction of Divine Love, grace, peace, and joy. It is in letting go of what has been blocking our connection to God that allows us to better hear our divine rhema, the unique word of Christ in our hearts. Examine your heart, observe your daily life to determine what or who has been preventing you from a full experience of Jesus as your North Star.

MY DIVINE RHEMA FOR YOU

The rhema spoken to me is meant for me to share with you, to show you that you too are able to listen to your divine rhema. It is my hope that some of these messages will resonate with you. Primarily, though, I hope you will be inspired to discover the divine rhema waiting for you when you rest and are in a state of "being" in nature, or quietly perceiving Divine Love in the world, our living sanctuary.

Earth, Our Living Sanctuary: A Messenger of Divine Rhema

I am immersing myself in the woods today. It is the end of summer, a liminal time. Mother Nature has peaked in her fullness. Trees have exploded with all the leaves they can create. Smaller plants, bushes, and flowers are competing for sunlight on the forest floor. I see butterflies everywhere I turn. I hear the babbling of the river. The river always has a message for me when I sit and listen. Nature always has signs for me when I align myself with the energy that is all around me. The earth is a living sanctuary. Not just a beautiful home for all of creation that resides here. Not just a majestic planet that we are encouraged to protect. She is so much more than that. She is a living sanctuary, reverberating with Divine Love found in every plant, flower, and animal. If we step away from our phones and computers, away from our televisions, and outside of our home, then we can become conscious that we are also part of the energy of earth as sacred space that, miraculously, communicates with those of us who listen.

Flowing Away Like a River

The days of the intermediary are flowing away like the current of the river. I can point to God. I can show you the/a way to God. But then I need to get out of the way and let you experience God on your own terms, knowing that an encounter with God is nothing short of an encounter with Love. An encounter with God is safe, powerful, and all-encompassing. God is waiting for you. God longs for you. Because Love wants nothing else but to be loved. Love wants to experience itself.

A direct encounter with God has powerful implications. Have you ever explored the many ways that we allow people, products, concepts, or cultural norms to come in between you and the Divine? It may have been necessary or helpful to have people be an intermediary, but those walls are falling down. They are crumbling.

God Speaks in the Quiet

Three times in the past few months I left my house for a walk, seeking quiet in nature after a house full of people or a noisy, full day. One time it was 8:00 am on a Saturday and I knew it would be quiet. I was wrong. I turned the corner in my neighborhood and workers were digging up a concrete driveway with drills. It was painfully loud! Farther down the street someone was blowing their leaves. As soon as I escaped some noise, another noise was right there. It was hard to escape! Even amidst the noise, the wisdom came in clear: We are entering into a very noisy time period. It's going to be loud "out there" in the world. All the more reason why it's important to go within to seek your silence and find it. Keep up with your quiet time, your meditation time, your quiet listening to God. Let it ground you. Prioritize listening to God in the silence while the world is noisy for the time being.

Emancipation from Obligation

What if obligation were taken out of the picture? If there are aspects of being in a faith community that feel like a burdensome obligation, then we feel guilty if we don't want to do them. What if not everyone feels the need to confess their sins every week? More and more, people's spirits are ready to be reminded that they are beloved. More and more, people understand that they are worthy of being called blessed. God said that human creation was good in Genesis. And yet one of the ways that churches can keep people tethered to them is by reminding them of their sin and error.

My child, you are beloved now. You are beloved whether you confess your sins every week or not. You are beloved whether you attend church on Sundays or not. You are beloved even if you don't love organ music. You are beloved if you find belonging in ways that are countercultural to a religious faith community. Because there is nowhere God is not. If your spirit is connected to God, and if you are open to paying attention to how connected and open you feel in your relationship with the Divine, then trust your leanings. Release the obligation of what any organization tells you that you "should" do. Your only obligation is to love, care for, and nurture yourself, the ones you love, and the community around you. What that looks like is up to you. Perhaps you are going through a time of deep personal growth, and you are craving time alone. The sound of music and a crowd of people feels like it is coming between you and the longings of your heart to listen in stillness to the grace and healing that God is sending you, quietly, and in God's time. Lean into that, my love.

Let go of that which is heavy. Release it. The Love of God should feel light and free. It should be unburdened. Your emotions and your movement are welcome with God. Cry, laugh, dance, sit in awe, walk, and pray. Forest bathe. Absorb the beautiful energy of love that reverberates through Mother Nature. Allow God to show you God's sanctuary. It is perfect. And you are perfectly a part of it because you are a part of Mother Nature too. You are perfect as you are to her. No membership or requirements. No dogma. Let her love enfold you. Quietly sit by a flowing stream and ask to be shown her wisdom. Watch the insects. Learn from the spider who spins her web perfectly. Her work comes innately to her. A perfect rhythm and flow, spiraling out. Release whatever obligations are bringing you down, even if just for a time, and soak in her Love.

Your whole self, as you are, is welcome to God. A faith community should model this unconditional love, free from burdens, free from anyone telling you anything less than that you are a beloved child of God.

Beautiful Weeds

What makes some beautiful flowers weeds while other beautiful flowers are sought after? Why is it that some flowers are loved by bees, are part of Mother Nature, and yet we kill them? We spray poison on them or pull them up. And then we go to a nursery to buy other flowers for our yards and do all we can to keep them alive. Why? Because some aspect of our culture told us how to think. People told us that flower over there is not wanted, and this other flower over here is wanted. Love doesn't do that. Love would never do that to people or plants. Mother Nature does not do that. What I want you to know is that you are loved. You might be a weed to organized religion but you are a blooming flower to God, and your bloom is beautiful. It doesn't matter to God if you fit in to organized religion or not. Let your bloom be your bloom. Be who you are meant to be. It's okay to stand out. It's more than okay—it's beautiful. Don't change your life or your appearance so that you fit into an organized religion. Stand out because you are beautiful as you are to God.

Removing the Societal Corsets

It is time that we go beyond our roles.

My pinky finger is a part of me, and it does not define me.

My left arm is a part of me, but it does not define me.

My heart and brain are a part of me, but they do not define me.

I am more than that.

I am a mother, a wife, a sister, and a daughter, but those roles do not, on their own, define me.

I am a writer, a speaker, an entrepreneur, a priest, and a faith leader. I am all of these roles, and yet none of these roles fully define me. Because I am more than that.

I am a woman, but even that is not all of me.

We should all be free to express ourselves fully and be fully ourselves without limitations placed on what we look like, what we say, how we dress, or who we love. The day of the corset is over. What invisible corsets remain in our society that we need to remove? How have you been limited, minimized, or encouraged to conform yourself to an image or role that is not you? Or that constricts you?

Remove the societal corsets! It is time to go beyond your roles and to expand your concept of who you really are. You are human and divine. And Divine Love is in your very being. Your very essence is Love, and Love is freeing, not confining. Remove the societal corsets and expand!

Freedom as God Intends

In integrating my Divine Feminine energy and allowing it to come forth and to strengthen, I'm allowing myself to release that which is unneeded. And I'm allowing myself to embrace that which is all of me. That is freeing! And doing that for myself means that I should also be doing that with other people in my life. So, I need to allow my spouse to be free, free to be who he wants. And my children, too. What could it look like to allow the ones I love to be fully themselves, and to allow that without judgement? I want to fully support the ones I love to have the freedom to allow all of themselves to come forward. This is freedom as God intends! My family is loving one another when we allow and support each other to be fully ourselves. A beautiful bird flew right across my sight when I said that aloud. Thank you, God in Mother Nature, for the synchronicity.

How Freedom Transforms Communities and the World

Why does any of this matter? A simple reason is that we enjoy life when we are not feeling burdened or weighed down by what other people, institutions, or organizations think about us. We can allow ourselves the freedom to be who we truly are. Can you imagine for a moment how liberating and joyous it would feel to have the freedom to be exactly who you are, without anyone else's judgement or expectation?

We are recovering the skills to unleash all of us, the Divine Feminine and the Divine Masculine aspects of ourselves. It is liberating to take off our masks and to allow ourselves to fully be ourselves, without concern for fitting into someone else's standards.

But ultimately, this matters because it allows us to help to make the world a better place. Whenever we see greater potential in us, and greater potential in nature, and when we see ourselves for who we really are, and Mama Nature for who she really is, and others for who they really are, then we are all being transparent and authentic in revealing our true colors. We can then more fully share the energy of love which is in all of us. We can transform our love, magnify our love, collaborate with our love, and share our love to make the world a better place!

When we dust off the film of muck (that is, societal conditioning) that was over our eyesight, and when we see one another, ourselves, and our earth for the wondrous creations that we are, then it allows us to see our gifts, assets, and ideas in a new way. We need to cleanse ourselves from the false narrative of what society says about who we are. Some institutions may benefit from hiding the truth of who you are. Because then they can sell you a product, a thing, or a person to fix you and get in between you and the divinity that is inherently in you and all around you. The truth is that there is absolutely nothing you need to do, become, or buy in order to be fully loved by God. You are inherently worthy of the love of God, the love of yourself, and the love of others.

The Emancipation of God from Labels

We are beginning to enter a huge cultural shift where people do not want or need anyone else to define who God is for them. People want to discover who God is for themselves and within themselves. Consider that the emancipation of God from labels comes after the emancipation of the self from labels. Often, an individual's understanding of God fills the container of their belief system at any given point in their life. When it is time to shed their understanding of God for something more expansive, it is often because their belief system has been expanding. Spiritual and personal growth come when we stretch our concept of God and self to go beyond where it currently is, to a greater understanding of Love. As our concepts of self and God stretch, it is normal to notice that we no longer need labels or anyone outside of ourselves (organizations/institutions) to define our relationship with God. This is a normal part of many people's faith journey.

Freeing Ourselves from the Matrix

> *"I'm trying to free your mind, Neo. But I can only show you the door. You are the one that has to walk through it."*
> —MORPHEUS, THE MATRIX

In the movie *The Matrix,* a blue pill will allow the hero to remain asleep and blissfully unaware of the real forces acting in the world, but a red pill will wake him up. Today, it's as though the blue pill is wearing off. We all took the blue pill, or perhaps the blue pill was forced upon us. But it's wearing off now, and we're starting to see that there's more to reality than what we have previously seen or experienced. Except that there is no need to take a red pill or another colored pill. The blue pill is wearing off, and it's a matter of looking around at a new reality—a reality that we haven't seen before. You don't need to take any pill; you simply need to be invited into a new understanding, a new way of seeing life, love, and God. It's far more beautiful than any pill, or any drug, or anything you can take to alter your mind.

Seeing this new reality begins with being silent and going within. There's a new world awaiting us, a new energy, and new possibilities. We have the power and sovereignty to not fall victim to the energies of fear and control, and to do that, we need to be open and aware that the new world is already here, and then consciously live into that. I have noticed that whenever I begin my day by saying, "I am awakening to the new energy of the present moment. I am open to the energy of Love in the here and now," then I can experience a spirit of ease and joy about my day. I experience things falling into place easily. By starting my day attentive (conscious) to the energy of Love present today, then I do not affix my energy to past pain or hurts, or future worries. In the present moment, the flow of Love is abundant and obvious, when we are open to experiencing it. This is Christ consciousness, being conscious (aware) of the love of God and the beautiful alignment that comes about when we carry this love with us throughout our day.

Hope for Humanity's Highest Potential

Once we see people for the Love that that they truly are, and nature as a loving home that has been truly alive as a source of grounding, rest, and communing with the divine all along, then we can join forces with the Love-in-all-of-creation-and-people to truly increase the reign of Love in our world.

Do you see how this totally changes things?

I am 100% confident that we have all the skills we need to eradicate suffering. We have the capability to eradicate hunger. We have the capability to eradicate poverty. We have the capability to cure disease. It is possible to alleviate most of our suffering in our world. Another way is possible! Allowing ourselves to *be* in and experience the energy of Divine Love is how we solve problems. When we understand that sort of energy and communicate within it and allow ourselves to play and be in a state of joy, then we will be able to eliminate suffering and solve problems in a holistic, collaborative way. That is how we can eliminate suffering.

I can't count the number of times I have been wanting to come to a solution about a situation or have wanted to figure out how to do something, and it's on a walk surrounded by nature that an idea "comes to me." When I am on a walk, I begin to refocus my mind on observing the beauty around me. I hear the birds sing; I notice how the flower buds are beginning to open; I notice the stage of life that the leaves are in. I notice butterflies, insects, squirrels, and hawks soaring. With my cognitive mind in a passive state and not actively controlling the situation I want clarity about, my spirit can finally hear what Spirit wants to say. An idea or creative solution drops into my mind and heart space fully intact. When I am experiencing being in nature, then I can hear Spirit so clearly, because the divine is all around nature. I can hear divine rhema and experience it through the signs and synchronicity of the world around me. This way of communicating with God is possible for anyone who is open to it.

In case it's not abundantly clear by now, seeking rhema is not navel gazing. This is not completely selfish. There is a higher purpose, and it has to do with your joy, and the joy of others, and the joy of our world. The way toward another possibility is through love. It begins with you. You loving all of you. When you see yourself for the truly wondrous being that you are, for the truly wondrous soul that you are, and that you are worthy of love, and that you are good, then you allow more of that to come through. When you allow yourself to see your divinity within, then it will also give you the eyes to see the divinity within others, and to see the divinity in natural world all around us. And once you have divine eyesight, all things are possible, because all things are possible with God.

All things are possible with love, and you will begin to see that love is absolutely everywhere. Open your heart and your Christ eyes to divine rhema and you will see a whole new realm and way of understanding. As my grandmother, my abuelita, said to me, "This will change you, my daughter." This is powerful, and it will change you.

Chapter 6
Reflection Questions:

- Recall a time when you have heard divine rhema (an example of God speaking to you personally). When did you hear it?
- Describe the specific situation that preceded you hearing it.
- Sometimes God chooses to speak to us in times of chaos. This time, was your mind overactive or were you in a state of quiet and openness?
- How is the metaphor of Jesus as North Star meaningful and inspiring to you?
- When have you felt like you were wearing an invisible corset—encouraged to minimize who you are for the sake of what society tells you that you should be, do, say, or look like?

7

A New Era of Divine Feminine Rising: The Return of the Divine Mother

INTERIOR REVOLUTION

A Glorious Procession

Blow the trumpets! Sound the horns! Lay down a carpet of spring moss and colorful flowers. Let the palms sway and the flags wave! The queen is here! The Goddess is making Her[32] entrance! She has finally arrived. She processes down the flower-strewn path, and we who have been awaiting Her arrival see Her for the Goddess that She is. Yet others will not see Her for who She is. To them, She, like other women, is nothing more than the vessel for a child. They will not understand the significance of Her arrival because She is *just a woman*, they say. But for the rest of us, our Queen of the Universe is here. She comes my way, Her regal gown flowing in the air. Her presence is gentle yet strong, emanating powerful love like an angel. As She approaches me, I lower my eyes out of reverence for Her. Out of deep respect I bow my head. She pauses right in front of me and says, "Raise your head, my daughter. Lift your eyes to mine. Look into my eyes: see your own image reflected in my eyes, as I see myself in your eyes. For I reside in each of you. I am *here*. *I am in each of you*. Your Queen, the Divine Mother, is here."

And I, in my smallness, am mesmerized by being in Her presence, but also afraid of what *they* will think. What would the people who know me think if I were to proclaim the arrival of the Divine Mother? How would they judge me and misunderstand me? What witch trials would I have to endure, yet again? I think of the worst I've been through and wince at what could come of me. I am afraid. But then I remember. I remember how Jesus held me in my mind's eye during the worst, and I know that his tender love perfectly included and integrated the Divine Mother. She was there, through him. And I recall the countless times I felt safe, loved, and nurtured in the wilderness that was my sanctuary, knowing that She was loving me through Mother Earth. I look back at my journey from strength to weakness to strength again, knowing that She has been with me all along, and within me, as I have come to recognize the divinity within me and others I encounter. She has been moving through the people that love me with warmth. Through them, she has supported my healing journey and she has compelled me toward compassionate action for others. She has been moving through the church when she is welcomed, however subtly. She has been there, quietly, all along. I consider how this world we live in is longing for a balance to unchecked patriarchy and sexism, unchecked corruption and greed. And I see, in Her radiance, that She is here to balance our lopsided reality.

She is the side of God that we have been shielded from. She is the aspect of God that our culture, our leaders, our stereotypes, our stories, and our archetypes have prevented us from fully knowing. She is Woman Wisdom, the Divine Mother, the Queen of the Universe—the missing side of God. Ultimately, Her loving radiance is larger than even my ego, held captive by fear of unknown potentials. I know then that if it is God's will for me to announce Her presence, I will do so. I see that we need Her to see the fullness of God, for God is more than He. I feel afraid some days about the reaction to my announcing Her presence, even though I know this is the right thing for me to do—to be honest and forthright about Her arrival. This is Her time.

I lay down my fear and instead reach for my horn. I steady my feet and take a deep breath to give it a thunderous blow. It echoes through the air, a sound of announcement and celebration being carried by wind that continues to this day, racing from neighborhoods to villages to cities, from country to country, across seas and continents, reaching far and wide, even to the farthest stars. Our Divine Mother is here, now! The wind delights in carrying this most anticipated message. It is with great joy and pride that I lift my horn to blow and wave my banners, I dance and twirl around as endless flowers, grown from the compost of old hurts, unfurl their fragrant blooms around Her. The forest awakens, branches swaying back and forth. All of nature rejoices as we announce the reign of the Mother of God! The Mother of the Universe, the Divine Mother, is really here!

Sacred Silence

It is in sacred silence that such visions, which I believe to come from God, can arise to our conscious awareness.

The sacred Scripture of the Divine Feminine is written on your heart and can be found through silence.

Silence experienced in nature allows one to hear that sacred Scripture and experience it in and around Mother Nature too, because her energy is also feminine. We allow her to awaken by resting in stillness because the Divine Feminine is within each of us. She is the interior divinity for each of us. She is the Goddess/God within each of us. We awaken to her through silencing the overactive mind. Because when we rest in silence and when we quiet and calm our mind, then our soul has a chance to awaken and to listen and speak. Then we can give our own wisdom the authority it deserves when it is grounded in the love of God. We can hear what arises through silence, which is love. Love is always what arises from the Divine Feminine through our silence. Divine Love is what pervades the entire world. Let nothing separate us from such Love.

Tokens

> *"For I am convinced that neither death, nor life, nor angels, nor rulers, nor things present, nor things to come, nor powers, nor height, nor depth, nor anything else in all creation, will be able to separate us from the love of God in Christ Jesus our Lord."*
> —ROMANS 8:38–39

If sacred silence, grounded in the Love of God, points toward our innate connection with God, then we are liberated from relying on outward tokens as signs. All we need is inside of us. That being said, when I go away on a spiritual retreat, I like to bring back a little token for my children. Perhaps a shiny stone that says Love or Faith, or a gold coin with an angel on it. Or a hawk feather I found, or a leaf in the shape of a heart. As we cultivate our children's understanding of divinity in the world around them and in them, it can be lovely to give them a little token to remind them that God is always present. If they are afraid of sleeping at night when it is dark, a little angel token can remind a child that they are safe and can always pray to God.

There have been many times in my life when tokens have brought me comfort as well. They can be much-needed signs of beauty and hope that God is near us. There is nothing wrong with beautiful symbols to remind us as adults too, that divinity is both around us and within us at all times. It is fine to have a little reminder of God to inspire and cultivate your faith if that is helpful to you. If lighting a candle or having a few meaningful objects helps you to create a space that feels like a sanctuary of love, then so be it. Know that there is nothing outside of you that is *required* for you to access the divine. If you notice that you are relying a lot on outside reminders, it may be time to remind yourself that the God you seek to draw near to can be found within you. In reality, you don't need any token, object, building, or outside symbol for you to be connected to God-in-the-world and God-in-you.

Once you fully believe, understand, and sense that divinity is everywhere, then outside symbols have no greater power than the divinity inside of you. In fact, the power anything outside of you has is due to the fact that you attribute power to it—and that is evidence of your ability to co-create your reality.

You assign power and significance to objects and people in your life. You decide.

Ultimately, divinity doesn't need to be seen to be felt. People, churches, and companies profit off of your desire to surround yourself with reminders of God found outside of you, so be mindful that there will always be efforts to sell you a closer experience with the divine. Remember that an experience with the divine can't be bought. All you need is inside of you and all around you.

This applies to more than faith-based tokens and trinkets. There is no stained glass, no statue, no stone, no incense, no candle, no place, no herb, or drug, or drink, indeed, nothing that can bring you closer to God than acknowledging that divinity is inside of you. Some quiet time and the desire to hear what Divine Love is saying to you is all you need to draw near to God. That can't be bought. Humanity has been searching for God everywhere and has tried everything. The answer lies within. The divine has been with you all along. You have divinity in you. When you don't recognize divinity in you, then you don't recognize it in the world around you, so you search everywhere for it. But once you truly understand that divinity is within you, then you can't help but see that divinity is in others, in nature, in the flower, in the stone, and all along the journey of life. Divinity is everywhere. There is no thing to purchase; there is nothing to obtain. From the perspective of the Divine Feminine, there is no pilgrimage to make outside of the journey within you.

UNLEASHING (DECOLONIZING) OUR CONCEPT OF GOD

The journey toward an interior revolution begins with an exploration of the attributes of the Divine that we were raised with, along with our experiences. There is a connection between decolonization, deconstruction, and the Divine Feminine. It is necessary to step back, deconstruct, and decolonize the belief systems we were raised with. By doing so, we allow new truths that were otherwise blocked to break forth like the sun. We analyze what was loving and what was not of love. We clear away the cobwebs and dust of that which was not liberating to our spirit. This allows us to better see the bright light of the Divine Feminine that has been hidden by our belief systems. We clear away that which we now see was harmful to us, not fully rooted in love of self and love of others. We choose to release it. It is no longer necessary. This allows a more expansive energy of Divine Love to pour through.

As we engage this process, we will see that the shadow side that has been repressed includes the beautiful part of our lives and our faith that doesn't neatly correspond with patriarchal Christianity. What beautiful parts of us need to be unleashed from the shadows?

Who Has a Clear Connection to God?

On a macro level, patriarchal religious institutions have suppressed the Divine Feminine. The Divine Feminine allows for the universal notion that divinity is in all things and in all people. Patriarchy has been upheld through multiple levels of authority and power. This partial understanding of the divine is rooted in the desire to find divinity outside of ourselves and to look outward to another authority figure who knows better than we do. This can function like a religious caste system, keeping up an illusion that religious leaders at the top have a clearer connection to God than those at the bottom. The truth is that every person has the same ability to listen to God in their life. No one is loved by God more than another person. In the eyes of God, no one is closer to God. The divine Mother/Father God loves all children equally. You are all capable of being connected to God if you choose that with your free will. I have repeatedly experienced awe when people share a glimpse of their deep connection with God with me while they wait in line at a food pantry. I know someone who cleans homes who has a crystal-clear communication with God. I know priests and bishops who are pure of heart and deeply connected with God. I have also seen church leaders abuse their power. People of all stripes live into all categories, whether they listen to God, choose to harm others, or put their ego above all else. No title can dictate who is able or not able to listen to the still small voice of God in their heart. Don't let any structure or institution tell you otherwise.

On a micro level, on a personal level, allowing the Divine Feminine to shine through begins with peeling away the layers of messages that you are consciously or subconsciously allowing to limit you. Is there a part of you that believes you are not worthy of love as you are? How are you trying to fit in or conform to a standard that is taking your energy, time, and money? What messages are you hearing that imply you are not enough as you are?

Releasing Suppression

I've been spending time in a forest on land that I know was home to the Cheraw people. I've been thinking about how, over hundreds (and in some cases, thousands) of years, Indigenous populations have been eliminated and suppressed. And African populations have been killed, oppressed, and enslaved. This suppression has happened in the name of God the Father. This is not Divine Masculine energy, which is not violent or oppressive. This is the ugly side of colonialism, empire, and patriarchy, which has thus far remained unintegrated from the Divine Feminine. We need to ask ourselves what aspects of our faith are still seeking to suppress people and ideas. Are there parts of our spirit or aspects of our lives that are suppressed as a remnant of being part of an organized religion that has in its systemic makeup—its DNA—the energy of oppression? The act of suppression was not blessed by God the Father. It is not of Christ. It is time to ask those hard questions and to deconstruct aspects of our religion or belief system which have been harmful to us. It's time to reunite with the energy of God, which seeks to liberate and expand. The energy of Love is freedom. The energy of Love is welcome. You are loved as you are. There are no prerequisites. There are no rituals or sacraments or rules that are required for you to be loved by God. It is the love of God that invites you to be love in our world. It doesn't matter how you make a living, or what you wear. It doesn't matter what you look like; it doesn't matter your skin color; it doesn't matter how much money you have. You don't need a bigger home, and you certainly don't need to follow a list of rules to be loved by God. You don't need to minimize yourself to fit into someone else's standards.

Take a step back and deconstruct and examine the belief system that you were brought up in. Take a close look at what aspects of your belief system you now see as harmful, and what aspects have been helpful. What messages did you hear from your parents and grandparents? What messages did you hear from neighbors and pastors and Sunday school teachers, from teachers in school and friends? What was rooted in fear, control or shame? What was rooted in love, wisdom, and the fruits of the spirit? Have there been aspects of organized religion that have been helpful and affirming in allowing you to embrace and love yourself? Have you experienced affirmation, liberation, and love? What messages have been harmful? What has been limiting to your soul, critical, or guilt inducing?

Take a good look at the belief system you were raised with, and then, with the divinity in you and with your full self, allow yourself to release that which you no longer need and stand firm in knowing that you are loved by God as you are. You are a part of Mother Nature, who nurtures and sustains your life. You are part of this beautiful creation. Awaken to that beautiful reality. Become conscious of that, because structure around divinity is not required or necessary for many of us to feel worthy of drawing near to God. That's why a lot of people are leaving organized religion.

Liberating Ourselves and Our Concept of God

We begin to truly thrive when we are liberated and emancipated from concepts that are limiting to our potential. When we consciously release family patterns, cultural concepts, guilt, shame, limiting notions of beauty and worth, and more, then we allow ourselves to be wide open to the expansive love that God intends for each of us. What is limiting you? What aspect of conformity has society sought to impose upon you that inhibits you from spreading your arms wide in full acceptance of loving yourself exactly as you are, now? Being conscious of what we need to release and what energy we want to allow is an ongoing journey. We begin to soar in our life when the cultural shackles fall off and we settle into the reality that we are fully loved as we are, by God, and are supported by all of creation.

It is inevitable that after we consciously explore what concepts we need to be liberated from, we undergo a stage of being liberated from those concepts of God that keep God small, contained, and fitting neatly within the parameters and confines of institutional religion. Decolonize your mind, your heart, and your soul! Does your concept of God quietly judge you every time you mess up in life? Does your version of God prevent you from fully enjoying life? Perhaps your God expects duty and responsibility and condemns abundant joy. Perhaps you were raised with a rigid understanding of the roles of women, men, and children. Perhaps your concept of God has you thinking that your miscarriage is a punishment, a house fire is a punishment, the loss of a job is a punishment. Perhaps you are afraid to take a chance on life because it's not responsible. Perhaps you don't strive for your passions because that was deemed to be selfish.

Think about and explore the limits of God that you were raised with. Explore the limits and then allow in a wider concept of an unconditionally loving God who calls each of us, as we are, beloved, and desires that we experience an abundance of joy.

Nothing and no one should exclusively contain and define God for you. Break open and expand the concept of God that you were taught. Remind yourself that a spark of the unlimited love of God lies within you, others, and all of creation. Freeing up myself and freeing up my perception of God will look differently for me than it does for you, the reader. The shackles and limitations that you place on God and on yourself (and that others place on you and on God) are different than my own. And so our journeys of what we are releasing and what we are allowing in our lives are similar, and altogether different as well. But we can accompany one another on this journey of liberating ourselves from limiting concepts of self and God. We soar in a spirit of ease and flow once the parameters have dissolved, through the power of love.

VALUES AND ATTRIBUTES OF THE DIVINE FEMININE

Compassion

What is the nature of Goddess energy? What is the nature of the Divine Mother? Who is She and how is She different from Father God? The most prominent characteristic of the Sacred Feminine is compassion.

Compassion is love that is so understanding that it often results in action to relieve hurt or pain. To cultivate that within us, we have to begin with compassion for the self, because once we see and honor that the self needs compassion, then that understanding allows us to be more compassionate to others around us. There is an active component to compassion. It results in movement, change, and tangible care. We feed the hungry, tend to the sick, practice self-care, and stand up for those who have been injured. Compassion is the love of a mother, who would do anything to comfort and care for her children.

Gentleness as Strength

Alongside compassion comes the characteristic of gentleness. Being compassionate for the self and others is carried through by a spirit of gentleness. We give grace to ourselves and others by being gentle and compassionate. Then kindness flows. We are giving and forgiving. It feels graceful. There is ease and flow of love towards ourselves, our family, and our neighbors. Do not confuse gentleness with weakness. The Divine Feminine finds strength through gentleness, not force. Love is like water; the gentle flow of water softens even the hardest of boulders. A gentle nature undergirded by the strength and power of love is a force that can bring about societal change we have longed for; it can move mountains.

> *"Love your neighbor as yourself."*
> —MARK 12:31

I've lost count of the number of times church leaders have mildly chastised "self-care" as selfish, while encouraging people to instead do the work of the church in their spare time, once again creating a dichotomy that doesn't need to exist. Growing up, I remember seeing the acronym J.O.Y. on coffee mugs and kitchen towels, reminding women, in particular, to put Jesus first, then others, and yourself last. At first glance, I get it. Yet the second commandment and Leviticus remind us to love our neighbor as ourselves. We can't share compassionate action with those in need when we don't value ourselves enough to show ourselves compassion too. How many women are weary from an excess of energy spent on the wonderful roles of parenting and being a spouse or partner as well as managing a household, a job, meal preparation for those we love, and our appearances?

The love from the Divine Mother begins with the self, and in that way, it is the opposite of a patriarchal understanding of church and society, which benefits from our servitude, often at the expense of our well-being, our creativity, and our potential. A patriarchal Christian understanding of God is Jesus, others, and then self. The Divine Mother wants you to begin with loving yourself because we are more deeply compassionate for others when we start with a place of allowing ourselves to be filled with love. We love others as we love ourselves. And of course, Christ abides in others and in us as well. We can consciously honor Christ by loving ourselves and others. I love the roles of parenting, being a spouse, and honoring my vocation. I don't need a linear acronym because I am sustained by a love that flows. My conscious awareness of Christ in me and my care for my self allow me to have compassion and care for others and to see the Christ that abides in them. This love flows in and out like the breath, like a never-ending cycle.

Allowing All Attributes of the Divine Feminine to Pour Through

It is necessary to rest in the embodiment of the Divine Feminine because Divine Love includes both masculine and feminine characteristics. We have not been raised to think of God as flowing and gentle, yet, let us welcome and allow in the notion that alignment with the Divine Feminine brings about an ease and flow in our life. Her grace is generous because She is compassionate and understanding.

She is within us, so of course She understands all of us.

Let us welcome and allow in the notion of God as moving within the natural rhythm of the Earth: as the saltwater tides move in and out, as the moon waxes and wanes, in the life and death cycle of animals and trees. Consider also that the love of Christ spirals outward, like the spiral fractals of nature, in an ongoing and expansive pattern, ever loving more and more. Imagine the possibility that time can be perceived as circular or spiral and not just linear. Open your mind and heart to welcome in a new understanding.

Let us welcome and allow in the notion of exploring God outside the boxes of denominations. We in the church have, at times, shamed and looked down upon others who do so. Love is wide, expansive, and free. It does not easily fit within doctrinal rules and human understandings. The Divine Feminine honors the creative expression of being open, not closed, to wider ways of experiencing God.

Let us welcome and allow in the notion of God bringing us wisdom from silence, from the inward journey, because we have been raised with the notion of God outside of ourselves. But we too, are a part of Mother Nature. We too are a part of the cycle of nature. We too need times of rest and movement, of fertile creation and giving thanks for that which we have created.

Let us welcome and allow in the notion of wisdom and intuition coming from the heart, rather than the over-active mind. Let us welcome and allow in the Divine Feminine attribute that alignment with God can be found with joy and balance, not only through duty and sacrifice. Let us welcome the notion of allowing what is good and expansive, rather than resisting or controlling that which makes us uncomfortable.

Let us welcome and allow in the notion of a God that nurtures and holds us with the warmth of a grandmother or mother. Let us welcome and allow in the world of feeling, emotion, and intuition as realms wherein God also moves. For too long our feelings have been looked down upon as a weakness, even though God has guided us through intuition. Let us welcome and allow in, with gratitude, the signs and synchronicities that God uses to communicate with us when we are open to seeing with Christ's eyes. Let us welcome and allow in the joys of collaboration and co-creating with others, rather than competing in our separate silos. Let us welcome and allow in the power and beauty of God's first sanctuary, Mother Earth.

OUR EARTH MOTHER

Earth, Our Living Sanctuary

Mother Nature is an incredible resource, spirit, and creation that allows us to ground and re-center ourselves to God as expressed through Earth. Recovering our connection to Mother Earth is grounding and an ongoing source of inspiration and rejuvenation. Endless insights can come from Earth because the cycle of life itself is endless. Even after death there is rebirth. Because divine energy is infused throughout all of creation, when we rest, listen, and learn from her, then we begin to learn nature's language. Mother Earth has her own language, her own way of communicating. For example, I can sit at a river and receive insights from the river. I can observe a hawk that comes into my field of vision just as I have been envisioning something, and I understand the significance of what that means. I trust that communication and am guided by it. When I lean into the communications I receive from Earth, the result is always a sense of alignment and unfolding of my dreams into reality. This is what many Indigenous people have experienced for thousands of years. When we became industrialized and moved to living indoors, many of us lost that. But it is possible to recover it! It does not require living outdoors. I can go on a walk in my neighborhood, a park, or a greenway and notice the trees, birds, flowers, and bushes all around me. That is often enough to sustain this connection.

When I take time to immerse myself in the forest and simply observe, I often receive a message that is right on time for my life. I call the energy to me. "I am listening, I am observing. Thank you for revealing the message I am to hear." And, without fail, when I open myself up to listening and learning from Mother Earth, I receive a message that is full of love, wisdom, and insight. I do not need a building or a membership or any set of rules to do this. I simply take time by myself, go into the woods, and listen. The Earth is a Living Sanctuary. Her teachings are endless. And when we enter into the synchronicity of all of creation, then we have the innate ability to receive just the right message for us at just the right time.

In my years as an ordained minister, I have observed that many preachers notice the alignment between the assigned Bible readings in the Church Lectionary (the cycle of lessons that are read each Sunday in many churches) and the current events that are happening around us. Similarly, many Bible study participants will acknowledge that the wisdom of the lesson they are studying is in alignment with their life circumstance. And yet the Bible isn't the only way that God speaks to us. The Bible or any holy Scripture, as sacred as they are, aren't the only ways that God shares wisdom. I have found equally wise, loving, relevant communication to come from my time in Mother Nature. The person seeking alignment of the God-within-them to the God-in-Nature can receive wisdom that is also meant exactly for them at that time in their life. One only needs time in nature and the open desire to be connected to the God that abides in you and the God that exists in all of nature.

The Great Teacher that is Nature is available to all of us, all the time. Mother Earth transcends denominations and religious institutions because she is God's greatest creation. She is the largest, all-encompassing creation of which we are all a part. To enter into communion with the way that God is in and expressed through Mother Earth allows us to receive wisdom for us in a timely, relevant and loving way that is full of gentleness and peace. In this way, we are connecting to the energy of God that is pervasive through the first sanctuary, the living Sanctuary that is Mother Earth.

She Speaks and Is Alive!

This I know to be true: Mother Nature speaks to those who listen. If you ask for synchronicity and if you ask for signs that you are on the right path, Mother Nature will come through. The energy that is your prayer is felt by the Earth we live on and she is alive! And then simply look for the signs. A hawk feather found right on the path you walk on as you imagine your next creative endeavor. A little ladybug that comes in the dead of winter as you are thinking about something small but important. The bear that comes to you in your dreams from time to time. Or maybe you've felt constricted in some aspect of your life, and you come upon the old skin of a snake who has let go of that which has become too small.

Mother Nature interacts and speaks with us in a variety of ways. I kept finding broken-open bird eggs when I started writing my book—a celebration of new life. I kept seeing cocoons when my writing felt like I was emerging in a new way. I kept coming across caterpillars before my cocoon phase. The owl sings or the vulture appears when death of one thing leads to the birth of another. The dove coos as a reminder to be at peace in all things. The changing of the leaves invite me to also reveal my true colors. Winter invites me into a time of quiet preparation. What would Nature say to you, if you were to listen? What synchronicities await you if you are open to the way that God speaks to you through the Earth? What do the cycles of the seasons, of life and death and rebirth, mean to you, in your life?

My Divine Rhema for You

I am here in the forest, asking for integration with the Divine Feminine, and what immediately came in was that when we are connected to Mother Earth we are being integrated with the Divine Feminine. Let us come to sense and understand that we are part of her (Earth) and not apart from her. When we care for Mother Earth and we receive from her and give to her with awareness (with consciousness), then we are innately connected. This is also an integration of the Divine Feminine.

Treat Her Right (Divine Rhema)

I sat down by the river, which was swollen with fast-moving water from torrential rain and floods. I began by saying thank you to Mother Earth. I was feeling grateful and deeply connected to her. But the immediate message that came back was that we, all of humanity, use her. We all use her. We use her in the same way that church and society has used women. Many women are used by certain men who climb from one position to the next to create their empire. Women often get stepped on, undermined, and disrespected, and the same thing happens to Mother Earth. We use her for our own wishes without consideration that we are a part of her—that we are intricately connected. In the same way, all of humanity is intricately connected to the women that they use and take advantage of. I could feel the anger from Mother Earth on this day. I could feel the desire and rising up toward a great rebalancing that is to take place for Mother Earth and for women. More flooding will be taking place. Not out of punishment, but as a part of a great rebalancing.

White Bread (Divine Rhema)

Colonizers (Europeans) made white bread because they separated out the hull from the wheat. The good part—the hull of the wheat—got stripped away, as opposed to whole wheat bread, which has all of it intact. They wanted to make bread pure and white by getting rid of the hull, which we now know to be the healthy part. They separated out what *they* deemed was good and not good. They separated more than just food, they made decisions about what was sacred and of God, and what was not of God as it pertains to culture, music, ritual, language, and worship. Colonizers deemed the ways of worship of the Indigenous people they colonized as wrong and even dangerous. What was separated out or wiped out depended on the denomination doing the colonizing. For example, Catholic missionaries succeeded in almost obliterating the language and traditions of Lakota people by forcing their children to attend boarding schools which sought to correct and teach *the better way*. Lakota children were punished for speaking their own language and practicing anything other than what the missionaries taught.[33]

Beautiful understandings of animal symbolism and meanings, an innate connection to Mother Earth, and an alignment with the natural elements were deemed not sacred. Today, many mainstream forms of worship do not include regularly gathering around a fire, or the use of drumming to cultivate our spiritual state of being, or an immersive experience in nature to enter into a state of union with our Creator. Christianity would do well to recover the wisdom of many Indigenous cultures in the ways that they honor land and God by being in nature. Instead, mainstream worship often chooses expensive robes and organ music with European hymns while disallowing a wider expression of what is holy. Like bread, we need all parts of the wheat stalk to be healthy. We need the wholeness of God, not part of God.

Since discovering how clearly I experience God in nature, I have realized that I don't want to be apart from nature when worshipping God. When I enter into a church, I feel separated from nature in a way that no longer resonates with me. Mother Nature is God's sanctuary. Recovering that has been important for my faith. I AM part of nature and I AM one with nature. Discovering God in nature has been an important part of my faith journey. These days, I receive wisdom from Mother Nature. I am going back to my roots. I don't want to be inside of a building to encounter God; I want to be in nature. It is where God is calling me. In some ways, I don't have too much say in the matter because the messages from Spirit come to me so clearly in nature and so clearly when I'm in community with others. I've discovered that the best part was left out, just like with white bread. I want to keep my connection to God whole and get back to that deep union, before the separation of sacred and ordinary. This is how Divine Love is calling me to decolonize my spirituality.

INTEGRATION

A Journey for Anyone

Integrating the attributes and characteristics of the Divine Feminine is a journey, rather than a destination. The very act of appreciating a deeper awareness and opening of our concept of God as new revelations, experiences, and synchronicities come to us in God's time (*kairos*) is a sign that you are developing your Christ's eyes for this journey and are beginning to integrate the attributes in your daily life. After a time of lament and deconstructing painful parts of our faith journey, it can be incredibly beautiful and hopeful to welcome in and integrate a more balanced understanding of God.

Allowing the Divine Feminine to arise in you is not for women only. All people have the potential to be fully integrated beings using both

Divine Masculine and Divine Feminine traits and energies. The Divine Feminine has been suppressed over the centuries; anyone can allow that energy to consciously arise within them.

Jesus Was Integrated

As part of our spiritual expansion, consider that other religions have a more developed concept of the Divine Feminine than Christianity currently allows. Hinduism has a well-developed understanding of Kundalini energy and Shakti. Kundalini awakenings allow in a more expanded, vibrant understanding of life and God, and often result in heightened intuition. Jesus was fully human and fully divine. And in that fullness, he embodied both masculine and feminine characteristics of the divine. There are profound similarities between Woman Wisdom in Proverbs 8 and The Word as described in the first chapter of the Gospel of John. And in 1 Corinthians 1:24 Jesus is described as "the wisdom of God", acknowledging the Word and Woman Wisdom to be one and the same. His life shows us what an integration of the Divine Masculine and the Divine Feminine can look like. He understood that God abided within. He often went away by himself to pray, strengthening his connection to God, even before miracles such as feeding 5,000 people. Jesus faced the shadow sides of humanity when others looked away. Jesus sought to co-create a world where the hungry are fed, the sick are healed, and love was spread outward in an ongoing way, all the way to you and me. Jesus embodied an integration of the Divine Feminine and the Divine Masculine like no other. While Christianity has taken some wrong turns over the course of history in furthering his teachings through manipulation, force, deceit, and control, it is the Divine Feminine attributes and the wisdom from within that can balance our faith and advance our faith spiritually in the years to come because these are the very attributes that have been suppressed, yet are beginning to come in stronger in the here and now.

As one on the journey of integration, I see signs of Christ, the Word that existed before creation, with every step I take.

Integrated Communities of Faith

When I first started Root Thrive Soar, I was not consciously trying to integrate Divine Feminine values. I didn't even have the words to say that. Root Thrive Soar[34] is both the name of my faith-based organization to support churches, and the name of the three-year journey I designed (co-created, with God) to accompany cohorts of churches from primarily doing church ministry inside the church building to increasingly being the love of Christ in their communities through compassionate action. Root Thrive Soar was co-created through months of deep prayer, listening to God, and my own lived experience of years of serving in humble yet vibrant communities. I can now see that we embody Jesus' values that are also Divine Feminine values.

Because they are Divine Feminine values, they are often missing, or weaker, in church culture today, even though everything Root Thrive Soar does is Biblically based.

Interestingly, many church members I work with come to me tired and burned out from church ministry. But when they become active with Root Thrive Soar, they feel energized, passionate, and joyful—this is definitely a process that nourishes the soul because the foundation lies in growing the love of Christ with and among others. This is not church committee work! Root Thrive Soar accompanies faith communities on a journey of deep listening to their neighbors. Congregants and parishioners receive training and support to leave their church buildings to encounter their neighbors for the sake of getting to know them, and ultimately listening for how they can partner with them to be a blessing to the community, together. We start by listening for how the Spirit is already moving in their communities. We listen for our neighbors' gifts, passions, hopes, and energy, knowing that God (Divine Love) is likely already moving in their lives. We spend time getting to know our neighbors without a spirit of conversion or manipulation. Rather, we strive for a genuine expression of the love of God in Christ. We emphasize *being* over *doing* (meaning that being in relationship comes first and leads to whatever service or ministry we will do together to serve the community). We seek to be in solidarity with our neighbors, which can mean showing up to community meetings, school gatherings, or lingering on front porches. Our compassionate action is the fruit of our co-creating with our neighbors. We don't do things "to" or "for" others, but rather "with" and "among" others, in a mutual way, meaning that we all benefit. The partnerships and collaborations that emerge happen with a spirit of balance, adaptability, and flexibility. If we feel stressed, pushed, or tired, then we stop. We take breaks, we make sure we feel a spirit of joy in our actions, and we honor the sabbath. In this process of showing up, deepening our compassionate action, our solidarity, and our presence in the community, both the church and the community benefits. Over time, both the church and the community thrive and Christ's spirit of love grows. This is a grounded, contextual process that bridges churches and communities, while integrating Divine Feminine values that have been left out of many aspects of patriarchal church today.

I AM

I AM opening myself up to a living relationship with the Divine Mother: the Divine Mother of the Cosmos and the Divine Mother in me. In the same way that we can have a living relationship with Jesus Christ, and in the same way that those of us who love Mary can have a living relationship with Mary, we can also have a living relationship with our Divine Mother.[35] It is utterly healing to cultivate this relationship. Even those of us who have loving parents experience times where we are hurting because of something our parents did, whether intentional or not. No parent is perfect. It is through the love of the Divine Father and the Divine Mother that we can heal core wounds.

How we encounter the Divine Mother or the Divine Feminine is directly correlated to what we're ready for, similar to an encounter with Christ. God, in all of God's forms, is ready to meet us once we say I AM ready.

If we want a personal encounter with God, Jesus, or the Divine Mother or Divine Father, then ask with an open heart and be open to receiving it. Or perhaps we are ready for a more nuanced encounter, or an encounter that is more integrated with the earth. Our free will and our open heart can determine how we perceive and encounter the Divine. The Divine Feminine can be met as a woman, as in the vision I had in the beginning of this chapter, or in a more nuanced way, as we deconstruct the layers of patriarchal conditioning. Perhaps we will meet Her by the river, in the forest, in the silence, or by looking in the mirror deeply. She is everywhere because God is everywhere. She is the counterpart to the Divine Father. You are not going to find much information about Her in Holy Scripture because She is within us. She is the embodiment of wisdom from within. This is not outward wisdom that can be found on the pages of Holy Scripture. Even the pages of this book exist to simply guide you to within, to discover your own wisdom. And yet by going within, clear visions of Her can come into fruition. Simply ask and you will receive what you are ready for.

I am on a journey toward experiencing the Divine Feminine in a variety of forms. My understanding and experience with the Divine Mother will, I hope, continue to deepen with time. Now, at this stage,

I am ready to proclaim the good news that I am experiencing a whole other aspect of God that, for me, coincides with being a Christian because I believe that Jesus perfectly integrates both feminine and masculine qualities, whereas our current version of Christianity emphasizes the Divine Masculine without the Divine Feminine.

My Initiation

After a long walk in the woods, I approached an opening in a forest, after both a spiritual journey and a physical journey. Spirit was showing me the beautiful way that my path was unfolding. With this awareness, this perspective of my journey, the only response was gratitude. "Thank you, Spirit, and thank you to Mother Nature, who is so full of divinity. Thank you, God, for this journey."

I intentionally slowed down as I walked toward the clearing in the forest, and it felt like an initiation into my awakening of the divine feminine in me. I am newly aware of the need for me to intentionally integrate the masculine and feminine characteristics of God/Goddess in me and around me, as Jesus did. For centuries now, God has been masculine or neutral at best. But that limits God and it limits God in me. I am new to this, so it does feel like an initiation of sorts. It is quite different from my ordination but this moment also feels full of sacredness.

But this time, I don't need fanfare. I don't need fancy robes. I don't need a church building. I don't need hymns. Here in the forest, I don't need a budget to make it happen. I need only to be fully aware of the holy that is all around me and nature, and to give thanks for it. I give thanks for the clear message which I allow to spring forth from the divine in me and all around me, which is the rising of the divine feminine. I give thanks for the clarion call to see the world fully, and to see myself fully, and to see others fully. I give thanks for seeing the importance of the integration of masculine and feminine now. I am able to see the divinity in all things now. I need only to allow myself to be still. To look all around me, and in my life, and to say like God said in Genesis, "It is good." I am so thankful.

I sit now at the clearing in the forest, quietly. I'm giving thanks for all the messages that I received and acknowledging this holy time. Immediately, I notice, in the clearing of the trees, one beautiful hawk emerges and begins to soar in swooping circles right over me. The hawk reminds me that Love soars. At the end of it all, Loves soars, with total ease. We are meant for ease and flow. We are meant to fly. We are meant to experience total freedom and joy. Goodness awaits us at every turn. Love soars.

Ritual

As you choose this new way of being in the world, it is normal and part of being human to want to create a ritual around this new beginning. If you want to light a candle and participate in a ceremony, then do that. If you want to get baptized as your way of following Jesus Christ in community with others, then you should get baptized. What I want you to know is that we do not do those things because God requires them, we do those things for ourselves. If you want to participate in a ritual, then choose the ritual because it's meaningful to you, not because you fear the repercussions if you don't do it. You are fully beloved as you are right now. There is no ritual, sacrament, or act that will make you more lovable to God than you are right now. The spiritual journey that God invites you into requires no specific ritual or ceremony to draw closer to God. You only need to desire that your divinity within you be awakened. If you are so moved by the incredible love of Jesus Christ and his life, and you want to follow him, and baptism makes sense for you, then by all means get baptized! But get baptized because you want to do it, not because you fear the results if you don't. Get baptized because you found a faith community to accompany you in life. Our God of love, that emanates in and through the world does not require baptism. If you experience being nourished spiritually from Holy Communion, then partake with gladness. God does not require it of you. Whether you experience worship in church on a Sunday morning as deeply meaningful to you or whether you prefer a walk in a park, or a sound bath, or a meditation, or a meaningful conversation with a loved one, then follow your heart! Know that God does not require anything of you.

Not everyone will agree with me about this, and that's okay. I stand by this divine rhema about where we are at this point in time in our spiritual evolution. And that is that there are no requirements besides your own desire and free will to walk this path. We are in a new energy and the love that is available to us in this world requires nothing, absolutely nothing to participate and receive love other than our desire to do so. Choose your rituals, your faith community, and the ways you express your love with intentionality and joy, but not because it is required.

In the spirit of the Divine Feminine, this is an interior revolution. It does not need an outside action for it to be true. You are loved by God, period. There is nothing you need to do to prove it to others. If anything, let your desire to spread the reign of Love in the world in partnership with others be the effect of the love that is liberated in your heart. Let that be the outward sign of the inward grace that you feel. Whatever you do, do so with a spirit of joy and love and because you want to. The days of guilt and coercion are falling away.

A Second Coming of Christ

The integration of the Divine Feminine leads to Christ consciousness. And Christ consciousness leads to the integration of the Divine Feminine. The two go hand in hand.

The second coming of Christ comes about when we gather up all the elements of humanity that have been suppressed and oppressed. We gather up the emotions, the feelings, the intuition, and the wisdom from women and so many others that patriarchal Christianity has left behind. We include the deep spirit of compassion and allow it to transform our faith and our lives. When we integrate the Divine Feminine, we acknowledge that the intuition from within us is sacred, too. The divinity within all of nature is also sacred. This deeper awareness is the consciousness of Christ. It circles back to the Gospel of John 1:1–3 when the Word was with us through the very beginning of creation and everything, *including the parts of us that were left behind*, came into being through the Word.

We cannot live into the understanding that all of creation came from the Word unless we begin taking a good look at ourselves. We were created from the Word, so let us recover the divinity in us, which includes loving and acknowledging our shadow side, the parts of our lives and personality that may have been oppressed and hidden. When we turn inward and acknowledge that *all of us* are included in the creation that came into being through the Word, then we come to a place of deep peace. This turning inward inevitably leads to a turning outward. It leads to the gathering up of all who have been rejected by society and/or the church. When we reclaim all of us, then it's easy to reclaim all of nature and all of creation.

> When we reclaim all the parts of us and of creation that have been left behind by patriarchal Christianity, we are actively integrating the Divine Feminine.

We are integrating that aspect of our heritage, our history, and our ancestry that has been oppressed, suppressed, and deprived of meaning. When we gather up all that has been rejected and oppressed in our wide, compassionate, strong arms and reclaim and proclaim that all of this, too, is divine, then we will begin to embody Christ consciousness in us. When enough of us gather up what was once left behind, then we do this as a society and a culture. This becomes the reign of Christ. This is the second coming of Christ.

For some, this understanding about the second coming of Christ will no doubt feel surprising, even shocking. Yet this was the message—the divine rhema—that I received so clearly one day when I asked aloud about the connection between the two. The entire time I received this message, I was looking at two hawks sitting side by side in a tree near me. The two hawks represented Christ consciousness and the Divine Feminine, which belong together. And as soon as I wondered whether to include the part about the second coming of Christ, one of the hawks left his branch and flew right across my line of vision. This beautiful synchronicity and alignment with nature (with the Divine Love that moves through out all of creation) affirms that it feels to me that this will be the second coming of Christ. It certainly has felt that way to me, when I have gone inward to bless and love the wounded, hidden parts of me that were rejected by patriarchal Christianity. I am not the first person to mention the connection between Christ consciousness and the second coming of Christ. Other spiritual thought leaders[36] have mentioned this before. As a Christian, I am experiencing it in me, the more that I integrate the aspects of the Divine Feminine that were wounded by church-operating-as-business. I experience Christ consciousness in me as I am drawn toward compassionate action with people on the margins in our society. And I notice it in me as I experience how I am a part of nature, rather than apart from nature. May it be so for you, too, if you are open to the expansion of your spiritual and faith journey to beautiful realities yet experienced. The second coming of Christ can dawn upon us when we align our prayers and compassionate action towards co-creating the Kingdom of God (the reign of Love) in our midst, in the here and now.

Reflection Questions: Chapter 7

- Reflect on the concept of the Divine Mother being a key aspect of God that we have been prevented from knowing. How does this resonate with your heart?
- What is it like to explore the notion that the Divine Mother is another side of God, of the Divine Father—without competition or threat, but rather one and the same (like two sides of the same coin)?
- Take some time to reflect on the messages you heard about God and church growing up from family members, friends, and church members. What was rooted in fear, control, or shame? What was rooted in love, wisdom, and the fruits of the spirit?
- What messaging do you need to release that you no longer need? What messaging are you ready to allow in, that you may not have received, or that is now new to you and you want to experience more of it? Take some time to release what no longer serves you and allow in what gives you a greater understanding of God's love for you and the world.
- How has the pressure to conform to societal expectations impacted your perception of God's unconditional love for you as well as your worthiness to receive God's love?
- What could the second coming of Christ look like for you?

8

Co-creating Your Life and Our World

What happens when an individual embarks on the journey to integrate the concepts of Christ consciousness and listening for Divine Rhema, while also integrating the Divine Feminine? What happens when these three seeds sprout, becoming more than theological concepts that live in the head, but grow to also live in the heart and soul, allowing these seeds to holistically take root in one's life? For me, it has meant an ability to co-create my life, partnering with God in shaping my destiny while seeking to deeply love my family and impact our world for good.

Restoring the Image of God as Mother and Co-creator

If we were made in the image of God then it would be the image of a woman who comes closest to the image of creator. The nature of our Creator is to create. It is to generate life. We all came from the womb of a human mother, and we have all come from the womb of the Divine Mother of the Universe.

We women can become life-bearers, can create, form, and grow humans. And although that may be the most obvious example of creation, the miracle of creating humans is often taken for granted. We also take for granted all of humanity's abilities in creating. We are co-creators by birth.

We are able to create worlds full of love. We are able to nurture thriving children regardless of whether we gave birth to them. We are able to create through pottery, paint, song, and food. We create through stories, symbols, and rituals. We are able to create collaborations, form ideas, foster partnerships, and dream new communities into existence. We are made in the image of God yet we have not been taught to cultivate our ability to co-create our reality, perhaps because co-creating draws us too close to the image of God as Mother.

I use the term co-create with intentionality. Co-create signifies that we are creating alongside God (Divine Love). The Divine Love in me is in alignment with the Divine Love in people and the world around me. When our love combines (when the God-within-me and the God-within-others works together), then we are co-creating. When we cultivate a living relationship with the Divine Mother (in addition to restoring or having a relationship with the Divine Father), then we experience a fuller understanding of God. And when we have a fuller understanding of God, then we can unlock divinity in us.

And once we unlock and expand our divinity to a greater extent, we can co-create with other people, heal wounds, and solve humanity's problems, because we are co-creating with the energy of Love—of God.

We are able to co-create ways to alleviate suffering and provide healing by our connection and alignment with our divinity within. This is why it is critical to expand our concept of divinity not only beyond the Father, but to us—within us and others as well. Our society longs for the alleviation of suffering and for us to co-create solutions. To do so, we must integrate the Divine Love moving through us and all of creation. This Divine Love is an energy that has lain dormant within many of us because we have not been fully conscious of it. However, the curtains are being pulled back now. The constructs of patriarchy are falling away, and new potentials are emerging. The energy in the universe is opening up in such a way as to make this journey easier and more accessible so that you take one foot forward in a spirit of faith and the path will start opening up and revealing itself to you. It is a most beautiful journey.

Jesus consciously lived as one who was both fully human and fully divine. The full divinity in him allowed him to master the integration of the Divine Feminine and the Divine Masculine. Additionally, he recognized the divinity within other people, as we see from the level of compassion he had for others. His deep understanding of his own divinity as well as the divinity in others allowed him to co-create the Kingdom of God (the reign of Love) wherever he went. We have that potential too. How many of us want the world to be a better place? We have the potential to partner the divinity-within-us with the divinity-within-others, to unite our love together for the sake of creating a more just and peaceful world. This is also following Christ. There is so much more to following Jesus than being good and doing the right things. It's time to go from playing checkers to playing chess.

A State of Balanced Living

It is the feminine energy of the Divine that generates new life, creative ideas, new possibilities, and new realms of potential. Any new idea that comes forth to aid us in restoring the balance of the earth will come from silence, balance, and/or a state of being, more so than from overwork. Divine Love brings us the ideas that humanity most needs through silence. The call to rest in silence allows us to be creative because the wisdom from higher realms—from Spirit—is then able to come forward so we can perceive it. This is the waning that comes before the waxing. The low tide that comes before the high tide. The Divine Feminine values being, resting, balance, and consciousness. We are part of a society that tells us that more work is the way to get more done. But by being in a state of balanced living, we can receive wisdom from the collective consciousness—from the Divine Love that undergirds all of creation.

In community we listen to one another's divine rhema—our wisdom received from God. Such wisdom often provides answers and creative ways of thinking. God does not want you to treat yourself as a machine. We are meant to honor the rhythms of nature, with ample time for rest and activity, stillness and movement. When we are aligned and connected to the sacredness of the earth, then we begin to perceive that the energy of Divine Love is not only in the earth, but in all people too. Collaborating with the Divine Love in one another allows us to co-create. When we co-create, things come into fruition with less effort, as we are manifesting within this flow of Divine Love. We can rest in the rhythm, the synchronicity, and the timing of Gaia or Mother Nature. The rhythm allows for times of rest and times that are slower. This is a flow that is of the Divine Feminine. It is not patriarchal. It's not about working more, doing more, achieving, striving, and getting things done. It is about resting and flow. It's about *being* in a state of trust rather than *doing* in a state of hustle, which allows what we co-create to come to us in God's time. This is the difference between God's time and our time. The rhythm of nature includes times of production and times of rest. Look at the plants. There are times that they produce fruits and times that they are dormant and resting. There are times that beautiful flowers and leaves are in bloom, and there are times when they look very bare. And in the same way, the flow of Divine timing (kairos, also known as "deep time") is feminine because there is a waxing and a waning. This is like the coming and going of tides and the wax and wane of the moon. There are times to rest and times to work. When we surrender to this divine rhythm that allows for times of rest and balance, then we participate in God's time, or kairos time. We lose our perception of chronological time as we gain a sense of the eternal now through Christ consciousness.

I would be remiss if I made the journey of co-creating sound like rainbows and butterflies. Thunderstorms and desert periods are part of life too, and God does not promise a life without hardship. But God does promise to be with us throughout our challenging times. I may have learned some keys to co-creating, but it's not always easy. I have struggled with just how long some things take, which eventually invites me into a place of deep faith. After the birth of our two sons, my husband and I hoped our third child would be a daughter. We were approved for domestic adoption and later realized just how hard it was to adopt. We prayed and envisioned and tried our best to have hope but after a couple of years, we realized adopting may not be the route for us, so we went on to try to have a third child. And then we had miscarriage after miscarriage. I stopped counting once the number of miscarriages I had reached double digits. I saw specialists, had blood drawn hundreds of times, and cried over each miscarriage. This went on for years. Finally I became pregnant with a baby boy who had Down Syndrome, with other complications. We met with several families who had children with Down Syndrome and did everything we could to prepare to welcome in our special boy. I loved him and felt fiercely protective of him. But when I was 18 weeks pregnant, his heart stopped beating. I was beyond devastation. I could imagine so clearly what life would be like with him. Still, we didn't give up. After seven years of trying, our baby girl came. She was a miracle in every way.

Even the process of publishing this book has led to co-creating. It took a year and a half for me to find a literary agent that believed in the vision of what I was doing. A year later, even with her support, I learned that Christian publishing houses aren't interested in a vision of church more expansive than their own vision, and spiritual publishing houses aren't interested in Jesus and quotes from the Bible. I had no choice but to part ways with my agent. I was on my own with a finished book, once again in exile. This time of challenge—of contrast—led to co-creation. I knew there were millions of people that loved Jesus but weren't interested in the boxes of Christianity, so I started my own publishing house, Contemporary Mystics Publishing,[37] after identifying this gap. Understandably, there are times that we can get anxious when what we want doesn't happen in our timeline. We are human and our faith falters. During these times I pray, "Lord, I believe! Help my unbelief."[38] In a stage of unknowing, when anxiety takes over, it's hard to listen to the quiet voice of Spirit. Sometimes that quiet voice says, "Wait and allow it to come to you" and other times the voice may say, "If you want it, create it." Co-creating is not easy and does not result in a perfect life or a perfect outcome.

We must also acknowledge that free will means that others we seek to co-create with have the freedom to make choices too. We often are not only co-creating with God. Other people and organizations can make their own decisions if they aren't an active part of your visioning process. So, what do we do when life feels like more desert periods or thunderstorms—when shaping our life is hard? I reach out to my community—to trusted friends and family. I give myself grace when I feel anxious or doubtful. I take time for self-care and self-compassion. All will be well, I remind myself. God the Father will not leave you. God the Mother will not abandon you. I want to be clear that sharing what I've learned about co-creating does not mean I have a perfect life, because I don't. This is not always easy, although there have been many times that I have felt at ease in this process, and I am not perfect. I hope that is clear.

However, I am able to say with joy that I have been practicing the following principles and have supported many colleagues and leaders as they practice them, for years. I started a church from scratch with others, using these principles. I've coached a growing faith community for those experiencing homelessness that used these principles. A vibrant young faith leader started up a joyful community in Harlem through envisioning and collaborating. Historic churches have become re-energized through collective visioning. Church plants have gained clarity and confidence about their purpose in their community. And an executive leader at a non-profit made inroads with the Middle Eastern community in their city and received support from their city council using some of these principles. These principles are faith-based and have supported practical, grounded expressions of co-creating our hopes of creating a better life for one another.

Over time, I have learned how to live a life of balance. I have learned how to be a co-creator in the most beautiful ways. I have figured out how to co-create a life rooted in love and joy. To be clear, when I write about co-creating, I am less interested in co-creating or manifesting material wealth as my primary goal, because I don't believe that excessive wealth leads to the deep, abiding joy that God wants us to experience. The co-creating I have experienced is one of spiritual abundance. It's a shift in how I see the world around me. It's a shift in vision that brings balance, peace, and joy. The co-creating I have experienced allows me to consciously see the way God communicates through synchronicity, resulting in the feeling of a deep alignment with the Creator and creation.

There are three spiritual/biblical postures and four daily patterns that have supported my ability to co-create. Consider these postures and patterns not as prescriptive but rather an invitation to try what has worked for me and others. I hope you'll also be open to what you may need that is not written in this chapter.

THREE SPIRITUAL/BIBLICAL POSTURES FOR A THRIVING SPIRITUAL LIFE

Before you learn how to unlock your ability to manifest love and joy in your life and in the world around you, it is essential to assess your overall spiritual posture, or your attitudinal stance with how you understand the way that God moves in and through your life. Most of us have passively developed our spiritual postures based on the faith we were raised with, the assumptions that developed over time, and specific life events. The spiritual postures that we have cultivated can and should be stretched and expanded to make room for a greater concept of what is possible. We want our spiritual postures to expand to make room for a God with infinite possibilities. Take a moment and ask yourself: Do I truly believe in my own ability to co-create with God? Do I try to have hope in difficult situations? What limits have I or others placed on my abilities?

1. **Notice and choose to follow the way that God creates.**

Recall that we are made in the Image of God.[39] God is our Creator and God abides in us. *As people made in the image of God, we are meant to co-create with God.* We are not meant to be passive recipients of life's twists and turns. We are meant for more than doing things "the right way." We can create a life full of joy, love, and balance. When I use the term "co-create," I acknowledge that I am creating with the God within me and all around me. I am connecting to the Love and divinity within as I create the life I envision for myself. In an effort to create a life of love and joy, let's recall how God began creating:

> *"In the beginning when God created the heavens and the earth, the earth was a formless void and darkness covered the face of the deep, while a wind from God swept over the face of the waters."*
> GENESIS 1:1–2

In the beginning, when God created, God created with a formless void and darkness. God needed a void. God needed space to create. In the same way, a painter needs a blank canvas before they paint. A writer needs a blank page before they begin writing. We cannot create with God when our lives are so full that we rush around from one activity or appointment to the next. We cannot enter the realm of listening to Spirit when we immediately turn on music or a podcast at the first moment of silence.

> *"Be still and know that I am God."*
> —PSALM 46:10

The journey to co-create a thriving life begins with our co-creating with God. And to co-create with God, we need to be able to listen to God, and we need some space in our lives in which God can move. When my daily schedule is so tight that I am rushing around with a sense of stress, there is no room for my spirit to hear God because my mind, which is in charge of doing, has taken over. But when I allow time to quietly be with God with my morning coffee, or when I have a walk outside with the intention of perceiving beauty in the world, practicing gratitude, and listening to the still small voice within, then my mind takes a back seat while my spirit co-mingles with the Source of Divinity, which is found in silence and in nature.

Without a doubt, numerous books have been written on this subject, but enacting this shift is key to co-creating with God. Cultivate space and room and then invite Spirit in to move. In the quiet, say: "Spirit, tell me what I need to know. Open my ears and my heart to hear you now and throughout my day. Help me to see the world with Christ's eyes."

2. **Notice, and then expand, the size of your faith.**
The second spiritual posture invites you to be aware of your faith. Do you believe that what you desire to co-create is possible with God's help? Stretch your faith! Keep it big! Notice how expansive your faith is. Your faith is like a channel that God moves through. If you have little faith in how God can move through you, then God will do a small thing through

you. If your faith is big regarding how God can do remarkable things through everyday people, then God will move through your big faith. Notice your own self-imposed limitations and notice the limitations that you put on God. Notice them, and then release them for a more abundant, more loving spiritual posture.

> *"I can do all things through Christ, who strengthens me."*
> —PHILIPPIANS 4:13

You have the free will to cultivate your faith. If your faith is small right now, you can choose to do something about that. Ask God to stretch your faith. Ask God to deepen your faith in God's infinite ability to move in your life.

Your faith in God's ability to move in and through you will, in large part, determine the breadth to which you can co-create and manifest the life of love and joy that you want.

Believing with the heart of a child that God can do wonderful things through you opens you up to be a channel through which the energy of God can move. In fact, no less than five times in the Gospels, Jesus referred to this. In varying ways, Jesus told people, "Your faith has.... healed you, made you whole, and made you well."[40] Jesus attributed the ability of his miracles to work in others' lives because of their faith. Children often are born into the world full of hope and faith. My children embodied a wide, beautiful faith when they were younger. Their beliefs are often full of fantasy and hope, imagination, and joy. One son, at the age of five, described a life beyond this one that is even more real than this life. Another son looked out his window when he was two and, in a quiet voice, described a beautiful sunset as a painting from God to us. My daughter's eyes dance with light as she describes angels with purple wings and magical fairies. She honors Mother Earth. When they are young, children can't help but dance to music—whether it's jazz in the streets or in a tutu twirling in the family room. They laugh abundantly with depth and pleasure, and it's normal for children to believe fully in that which they cannot see but can feel. To be around children, noticing their wide perspective and faith, is to experience the magic of the Divine. It's no wonder Jesus asked us to become like little children!

3. Notice, and then expand, your definition of "prayer."

In this third spiritual posture, we reassess our understanding of prayer. For most people, our notion of prayer means a petition to God. Traditionally, our prayer can be one of thanksgiving, a request for help, adoration, or stating a hope or wish for a situation or person. In our culture, prayer means we are praying with words, whether said silently or aloud. However, the Bible shows us that when we take time to envision what we want, we can aid God in making that a reality.

> "Write the vision; make it plain on tablets, so that a runner may read it. For there is still a vision for the appointed time; it speaks of the end and does not lie. If it seems to tarry, wait for it; it will surely come, it will not delay."
> —HABAKKUK 2:2–3

If praying with words is a one-dimensional prayer, then praying through visioning is multi-dimensional. Use your emotions and your imagination when cultivating a vision of your prayer request. Do you long to live a life of balance and peace? What does that feel like? Dwell in the emotion of your prayer. Perhaps you want to pray for love to flow to you and through you and to others. What does that feel like? Are you full of joy? Can you linger there? How can you make your hopes and prayers feel alive through the power of envisioning?

Conversely, worry can also be an unintentional way that we affix our mind and thoughts toward all that can go wrong in a situation. When you notice yourself worry about a situation, let it go, and choose to allow in a vision of a better outcome. You have agency to choose the vision you want, to choose the better thought. What is the most wonderful outcome that could happen? Imagine that for a while. Linger in the feeling of relief, the surprise, in the gratefulness. In many situations, our thoughts can be powerful. If I am thinking negatively about a person while worrying about an impending conversation, then my interaction with them will almost certainly be impacted by those thoughts. But if I allow myself to be open that I may not have a full perspective about a person and I'm open to the best outcome of our future conversation, then chances are, I've opened the door to a better outcome. To be clear, I do not believe that when bad things occur in our lives, it is because we didn't co-create the right way or think the right thoughts. Diagnoses, health challenges, car wrecks, and lost jobs are a part of life and there is no magic wand to avoid hardship. However, I have learned that there are times that my thoughts can impact an outcome, so I strive to be open to the highest outcome. This is why starting your day connected to God, conscious of your intentions is a proactive way to begin your day with your thoughts and feelings rooted in love.

When Jesus prayed in John 17, he began with himself, then those closest to him, the community around him, and finally, the world. In a matter of minutes, we can start our day envisioning love, joy, peace, and abundance for ourselves, our household, our community, our nation, and the world. Pray with your whole heart, your whole mind, and your soul.

It will take some time to notice the three spiritual postures in your life and to expand your normal frame of mind to more fully welcome in greater possibilities that are rooted in the love of God. Come back to these postures again and again. Think about them at the end of each day or week to assess how you are doing in stretching beyond where you were.

In addition to the three spiritual postures, there are four daily patterns that are more concrete ways to align yourself with the ability to co-create your thriving life rooted in God. You will notice that some of the patterns are a natural complement to the spiritual postures. They all fit together, like a tapestry, to support your spiritual expansion.

FOUR DAILY PATTERNS FOR CO-CREATING YOUR THRIVING LIFE

Pure love is the energy that God can do anything with. We have the ability to call the energy of love to us. It is time to uncover the power that every individual holds in co-creating our lives. It is time to recover the synchronicity and flow of being in alignment with the energy of pure love that reverberates through our earth. When we are aligned with this energy and aware of the fact that we have the ability to float with this energy, then it feels like we can shape the destiny of our lives. Over the years I have practiced these four daily patterns that I am sharing with you. Over time, it feels like I'm beginning to learn how to fly. Admittedly, it can feel a bit shaky at first. Can you imagine being a new bird spreading her wings, learning to go the direction you want to go? It can feel a bit unnerving as you practice going high, making a turn, slowing down. Stay with it, though, and you too can experience the ease and flow of flying, of experiencing the thriving life you are co-creating with God, filled with a spirit of love, ease, and joy. Manifesting and co-creating the life you seek to live is empowering and joyful. It is also, I believe, our birthright. We are meant to be co-creators. We are made in God's image of a Creator. If God is Love, then we are meant to call the energy of Love to us. We are meant to co-create our lives and co-create a world that is full of love: love for ourselves, love for others, love for our communities, and love for the world. The following four daily patterns have become essential to my ability to co-create a thriving life that is rooted in God/Divine Love. Perhaps, over time, you will identify other patterns that are essential to you.

Daily Pattern 1: Start the day with intention setting as a spiritual practice.

Intention versus Goals

Co-creating our ideal life is easier once we make the shift from achieving goals to creating intentions. I have been practicing co-creating with intentions for several years now and can attest to its power in shifting me to where I want to be.

A goal is about getting something done. For example, I may have a goal to walk five times a week and another goal to complete a project in two weeks. We can have goals like finding a job, lowering our cholesterol, or spending more time with family. A person usually writes their goals down, and it is on them to make the goals happen. It requires effort, and in many cases, work. If I need to reprioritize my time to meet a goal, then I need to look at both my calendar and my responsibilities. When I accomplish a goal, then I am lauded for my work ethic, for my determination, and for being a do-er.

When I am making an intention, I am focused on the spiritual posture or attitudinal stance that I want in my life. So, rather than say: "I will exercise three days a week," I say, "I am healthy and fit." Rather than say, "I will do all these things on my To Do list," I say, "I am feeling a state of flow with my job." If I am struggling to forgive someone and am thinking about it more than I want to, then, in addition to praying for that person and praying for God to help me forgive that person, an intention might be, "I am releasing lingering resentment. I am already forgiving them. I am welcoming in a spirit of peace and forgiveness in my heart." And, more than saying these things, it's noticing a shift in being and becoming what we seek, rather than simply doing another task.

I AM: Defining and Intending Who and Whose We Are

In the Bible, the Creator of the Universe is self-defining. God uses the phrase, "I AM" to define and clarify who God is and who God is not. "I AM the Light of the World," "I am the Resurrection and the Life," and "I AM the Bread of Life" are a few examples. There is immense power in naming who we are, too. As God's beloveds and as people in whom God abides, we too should claim our I AMs. In this way, we can co-create with God. When we define who we are and claim it, we become it.

I AM a beloved child of God.
I AM living a life of balance and joy.
I AM thankful and generous.
I AM worthy of being surrounded by meaningful, loving relationships.
I AM sustained by laughter and delight.

Consciously notice how you think and speak about yourself. What thoughts come forth when you look at yourself in the mirror? Are you affirming of yourself or critical? Do you see yourself as beloved? We should be mindful of the messages we say to ourselves throughout the day. Are you as affirming and encouraging of yourself as you are to your children or your pets? Do you look upon yourself with a soft heart and compassion towards all of you—your shadow side and the outward side that you show others? Before we co-create the life we dream of, we need to recover ALL of who we are as we claim our I AM affirmations.

Set your intention. Call the energy to you. Use the wording that God uses in Holy Scripture: I AM. I AM surrounded by love, flow, and joy. I AM serving God in others to the best of my ability in ways that bring joy and love to myself and others. I AM living my life full of vitality and confidence. I AM on the path where my gifts are best utilized for the higher good.

When you set your intention, do it with your full self. Don't just say the words; *feel* the words! What emotions come to you? Allow your heart to fill with joy as you imagine what a life surrounded by love, flow, and joy feels like. Imagine the passion and energy you feel when you are serving God and others in ways that fill your life and others' lives with joy. What does it feel like to live your ideal life? What does that look like to you?

Reclaim the Power of Your Feelings

I have found that the best time to sit with your intentions is in the morning, at the start of the day. You can either write down several intentions that are relevant to this stage in your life, or you can, each morning, simply intend how you want your day to go.

The key to practicing a life with intentions is to take time to feel them. If I say, "I AM experiencing joy with my family," I want to imagine the joy I want to experience with such vividness that I actually feel it! I imagine playing a game with my children and we are being silly and laughing. I imagine a Saturday afternoon chasing them in the backyard or finding shapes in the clouds. I imagine having time to read a book and savor the delight of an easy day.

If I say, "I AM experiencing ease," then I imagine a workday where I feel a spirit of ease throughout the day. I write a proposal effortlessly and the goals I have for a project come to me clearly. I have easy conversations with everyone I encounter. Rather than viewing my emails as taking up my day, I imagine that I do what needs to be done with ease and joy, and when my day ends, I feel a spirit of satisfaction.

While it is ideal to sit with intentions in the morning so that your day can unfold with the lovely energy of what you intend, it is also an effective way to re-orient yourself. If a day feels stressful and cumbersome, or if things are bothering you, go outside for a short walk. Take some deep breaths. If you can be around nature and trees, notice the abundance that

God shows us through Mother Nature. As you walk, intend the shift that you want to make in your attitude and being. "I am already letting go of this situation. I am at peace. I am compassionate. I am moving forward. I am deeply grateful for a new perspective. I am trusting of God."

This is the secret you will discover after practicing co-creating your life with intentions: It is easier to obtain that which you desire by feeling the desired emotion while lingering in the vision of it than it is to work to achieve the goal with your mind and intellect, while not using the power of your feelings.

It is easier to co-create when your feelings, your emotions, and your mind are in alignment through the power of your intention than it is to just work hard at a goal. Intentions bring about what we desire more easily than goals because with intention setting, we allow ourselves to be in alignment with the divinity in the world around us. We release control of details like how it happens and when because we are co-creating within the flow of life.

The power of our feelings and emotions has been largely unknown to us because our patriarchal society has diminished and belittled the importance of feelings while over-emphasizing the importance of the mind and intellect. Yet, recovering and allowing all aspects of ourselves to work together in harmony allows us to enter into alignment with the Source of Divinity (Divine Love) that pervades all the earth. When we sustain our thoughts and feelings toward that which we desire, we draw the energy to us.

In physics, "The Law of Conservation of Energy" states that energy cannot be created or destroyed. It can only be converted (changed) from one form to another. When we focus our energy (thoughts, feelings) on that which we intend, we call the energy into becoming matter. This is a law of science. It is how the world works. I have started a church with a thriving food pantry dedicated to serving the local community with this principle. I also started a successful faith-based enterprise with this principle. It works with smaller intentions and larger intentions. But here is another secret: since the energy of Love (God) is what moves through us and all of creation, then intentions rooted in Love come about with the most ease.

Daily Pattern 2: Visioning with the energy of Love.
Habakkuk 2:2 says, "Write the vision; make it plain." There is great power in visualizing that which you imagine. And, more than visualizing *what* you want to unfold in your life, visualize how it feels once you have already experienced the desired results. How *does* that feel? Fill your heart and mind with the feeling and emotions of it.

Do you see what's happening here? I am telling you to recover ALL of you in how you co-create. For too long, society has taught us that intellect is more valuable than emotion. For too long, a patriarchal society has shaped the belief that feelings and emotions are flimsy and weak and intellect and rational thinking are strong and stable. But a new day is dawning and more than anything, trust this: the mind is a tool of ours but should not be our primary tool. Because we can't think our way closer to love. We must feel our way there. And in order to enter into the flow of the living sanctuary that is all around us, we must recover the beauty and innate goodness of our feelings—all of them—and use them to envision a better way.

Since love is the energy that moves through you, me, and all of creation, one of the key pieces to co-creating our dreams is to envision how love is moving through what you want. For example, when I was creating a parachurch organization to help churches shift to being the love of Christ in the world through compassionate action, I would envision the love that mission teams felt from one another and the community. I envisioned the ways that the community and the church were connected in a spirit of love and were doing good works to improve people's lives in that same spirit of love. As I am envisioning this, I am not only seeing it, but I'm feeling it. I'm feeling love in my heart as I am observing (through my third eye or imagination) love spreading from all of the practitioners of the Root Thrive Soar journey to the community around them. I imagine the stories that participants are sharing with one another during our seminars and the love that flows from them to their neighbors and community members. I envisioned it and, in God's time, with the participants visioning it too, it came into being.

This envisioning doesn't just have to be related to our jobs, of course. Say it's been a challenging school year and it's time to plan a summer vacation for your family. Spend a few minutes envisioning what the best summer vacation would feel like, with a spirit of love and joy. Can you imagine the delight on your kids' faces as they play at the beach, splashing in the waves or at the pool? Can you envision the deep sighs of peace that come from a quiet moment in the mountains with the sunrise and your morning cup of coffee? Or the moments of connection that you experience with your family throughout the week? Can you imagine driving home from a full week away with your heart full of gratitude as you recall the fun, the delicious food, the family time, and the beautiful nature all around you? When you spend just a few minutes a day envisioning what you desire, in a spirit of Love, then the energy of love that pervades the universe will rise to honor your intention. And the more you can use your feeling, emotion, and heart in this process, then the stronger your energy will be, and it will be brought to you.

> *"Ask, and it will be given to you; search, and you will find; knock, and the door will be opened for you."*
> —MATTHEW 7:7

Ask and you shall receive: invite Spirit to bring you the lessons that you need to learn and watch them come to pass. Notice what comes your way once you intend to learn from Spirit: the movies, the songs, the conversations, the insights that you have on a walk. Try to be conscious of what's coming your way, rather than just being in the middle of it unaware because you have so much going on and you're going from one thing to the next. When you choose to slow down and be conscious, then you will notice that when you ask to go deeper in your insights, when you ask to receive the next lesson or the next spiritual awareness, it will be brought to you. For this to happen, we need to be mindful and aware of what is happening. It is incredibly validating and inspiring to see the way the universe brings it to you. Ask and you shall receive! Seek and you will find! Knock, and the door will be opened to you.

Daily Pattern 3: Go on a Spirit Walk in Nature or practice *being* over *doing* in Nature.

To live a life of balance means to be in synchronicity with Mother Nature. Not in power over her, but as one of the many living beings who reside here. When we spend time in and around nature, with the open intention of rebalancing ourselves, then we can become reconnected with the earth and the energy of love that is contained in all of life.

Whether it is a morning walk, an afternoon hike, sitting under a tree, grounding in your backyard, a casual walk in a park, lying on the grass and watching the clouds, or swimming in the water—in each of these ways and more, we can reconnect with the energy of the Creator. The energy of Divine Love resides in every blade of glass, every flower, every tree, and every insect. Immerse yourself in nature as you seek a return to a balanced way of life, in partnership with the Earth. You too will discover beautiful lessons from the Divine.

I have found that being in nature is a key daily pattern to my thriving life. If possible, I go on a spirit walk. This may be a twenty-minute walk in my neighborhood. It may mean ten minutes in my back yard, or a few minutes gardening and watering plants. I call it a spirit walk because I am intentional about quieting my mind and listening to Spirit. I can be among the trees and attune myself to the sights and sounds all around me. I have a full-time job, three children, and a spouse. As one who lives a full life, I have found that twenty minutes a day outside on a walk, aware that I am immersed in God's sanctuary, is enough to bring me balance, love, and insight to whatever concerns are on my heart. There's so much to nature that we can miss in our hurriedness so the time I am in nature is sacred time. She is the most beautiful sanctuary. She is more beautiful than muraled walls, gold painted ceilings, and Renaissance works. To be in nature with the spirit of receptivity is the equivalent of opening sacred scripture because we are in the divine presence of God in God's sanctuary. I find endless meaning in the significance of the various stages of nature: the potential of an acorn, rushing water, decaying leaves. These are icons in and of themselves, worthy of being seen with our Christ eyes.

Nature can show us wisdom that spirals and expands when we observe how Spirit moves through all of creation and is innately part of her essence. How does the stage of life that nature is in correspond with the stage of life you are in? Where do you find alignment with nature's cycle of life and death, waxing and waning, blooming and bareness? Christ consciousness means being present in the here and now and noticing the way that God is moving in my life at all times. When I sit in silence or go on a walk, both of which are forms of meditating, I am uncoupling the spirit from the mind. It is my spirit that guides me toward insights, revelations, and spiritual lessons that tend to spiral back around from time to time.

This is what came from me—from my soul and from divinity moving in me when I ask for guidance and then go into the woods to listen. So, the question becomes, "What is God saying to you?" When you linger in nature as a sacred space and bring your confused heart, you will find solace. When you have a concern and you enter into this greatest of sanctuaries asking for guidance, it is possible to hear it. And more than our personal problems, even our specific role in the solutions to the problems of our communities and the world can be heard when we quiet the mind and listen to the quiet inner voice of Divine Love. So, imagine what can result when many of us prioritize listening for our specific role and purpose to the wider problems of the world. You, who are passionate about the environment, what will you hear in the silence that can benefit us all? You who are passionate about medicine, you who are passionate about mental health, you who are passionate about poverty, you who are passionate about the well-being of children: What answers to our most pressing problems will come when *you* rest in silence? What wisdom will come when you listen to what Divine Love is saying through Mother Nature? What is Divine Love saying in an expanded way to you, in a way that spirals out and includes all of humanity and the cosmos?

I've learned over time that in order to be in synchronicity with Mother Nature, I can't operate with the notion of having dominion over her. Power over is not synchronistic. Nature's signs cannot be seen or felt when one perceives the natural world as something to control. Even the notion of "protecting" her is a form of power over. She is more powerful than all of us. If we enter into her flow and listen to her, she will tell us how to thrive, and how she can thrive. I am one of many of her children. I am one of many beings that is a part of the natural world. I enter into the cosmic love of nature with the desire to walk, move, and dance among her. I learn from her ways, like a child at the feet of her wise grandmother.

And always, when you leave nature, give thanks for her. Give thanks for the divinity flowing through her. Leave with quiet reverence as you enter with quiet reverence. Give thanks for the wisdom you have received, for the lessons you have learned. Take time to write the wisdom down and incorporate it into your day, your week, your month, and your life. Keep a spirit journal to write down the wisdom and insights you receive in the quiet. The very act of writing this down affirms that you value the insights coming to you. And looking back on what you write allows you to see the patterns of how God speaks to you.

Daily Pattern 4: Practice compassionate action with everyone you come across, including yourself.

This section is shorter, not because it is less important, but because compassionate action is so important that it is mentioned throughout this book. Compassionate action allows us to tangibly share the love and compassion within us so that the reality of another has been changed for the better. Any action toward another being is an exchange of energy, an exchange of Divine Love. When I give my time to serve those in need, it feels good to my soul to share my compassion in a way that results in food for them, a warm smile, and encouragement. Without a doubt, I receive more from them than I give, for I am often at the receiving end of a tender conversation, a funny moment, and a spirit of gratitude. Standing in solidarity with others is a tangible form of compassionate action because we align our energy with another in a spirit of justice and encouragement. When I am on the receiving end of compassionate action, I feel understood and cared for, that I am not alone. It may not be realistic to feed the hungry every day, though I fully believe that serving among those who are imprisoned, sick, hungry, or homeless in a regular way is a tangible expression of honoring God and serving in our community. We can practice compassionate action with our community, colleagues, groups of people in our society, the people we live with, our pets, our plants, wildlife near us, and even ourselves on a daily basis. If one of my children is irritable and acting out, I have noticed that if I pause to imagine what is happening inside of them with a spirit of compassion before I respond, then that energy of Love shifts their behavior much more effectively than if I quickly react out of impatience. And in order to be in the presence of mind to pause and choose compassion, I have learned that I need to begin my day with quiet time with God, filling my own heart with compassion and love first. Starting my day with God allows me to first receive Divine Love, allowing myself to have more grace towards those who need compassionate action in my household, my community, and the world. I could not have created and supported faith communities rooted in compassionate action unless I first took time to be compassionate with myself and my family. The energy of love should flow from person to person, creating a positive ripple effect that is ongoing. The ripple effect of God's compassion is ongoing to this day among people of faith inspired by the teachings of God as well as incredibly caring people in the world. God can move through us all. While aspects of our culture seem selfish or narcissistic, with energy and attention going to oneself, compassionate action invites us to give and receive love from one another. Compassionate action towards others is a tangible way we can improve our lives and our world and no action is too small or humble.

These three spiritual postures and four daily patterns provide a basic foundation to co-creating a thriving life, rooted in the love of God.

Living in Alignment with Love

It is time to uncover the power that every individual holds in co-creating our lives. It is time to recover the synchronicity and flow of being in alignment with the energy of pure love that reverberates through our earth. When we are aligned with this energy and aware of the fact that we have the ability to float while this energy sustains us, then it feels like we can shape the destiny of our lives. It feels like flying.

Manifesting and co-creating the life you seek to live is empowering and full of joy. You were made in the image of our Creator. If God is Love, then we are meant to call the energy of Love to us. We are meant to co-create our lives and co-create a world that is full of love: love for ourselves, love for others, love for our communities, and love for the world. There is nowhere God is not. There is nowhere Love is not. It is up to us how we recover it, increase it, and use the power of Love for the benefit of ourselves, humanity, and our beloved planet. "All things are possible with God" (Matthew 19:26). All things are possible with Love.

Our spirits are thriving when we are in full alignment with the Love of

God in us and around us. We begin to notice synchronicities in our life, from signs in nature, animals, and clouds; from people, music, and more. Most people think thriving is the goal to aim for. But beyond thriving, there is soaring. When we intend to partner with others who are also in alignment with God, for the good of the community around us, and when we are in alignment with the Divine Love-in-them and the Divine Love-in-us, a high form of collaboration begins to take place.

Collaboration for the good of people and the world around us is a sign of soaring in partnership with others. Since we are in alignment and flow with the energy of Love that exists in us all, things fall into place with ease and flow. When people's hearts have good intentions, when our egos and minds are tools but never the master, and when a spirit of Love is allowed to reign, then we will experience the ease of a hawk or eagle soaring, catching wind gusts that make co-creating effortless and full of joy. This is the reign of Love and the reign of God in our midst. This is in our field of potential! Believe it, envision it, and then reach out in your community with a spirit of Love. It is time to awaken to the possibility of soaring.

Chapter 8
Reflection Questions:

- Have you experienced co-creating? What did it feel like to co-create something you desire?

    First posture: As people made in the image of God, we are meant to co-create with God.

- Without judgement, assess whether your current life allows for space to listen and notice the way God is moving around you and in your life.

    Second posture: Notice, and then expand, the size of your faith.

- Identify a time in your life when a limited belief may have limited the outcome.
- Identify the times in your life where having a bold faith resulted in a big shift in your life.

    Third posture: Notice and then expand your definition of "prayer." Take time to reflect/vision.

- What would it look like to take five to ten minutes each day to pray/envision/meditate in a multi-dimensional way, using all of you (your mind, your heart, and your emotions). What commitment can you make to yourself to begin this life-changing posture?

PART THREE: SOAR

An Expansive Christianity—The Future Is Now

9

A Vision of Future Church

Envisioning and Co-creating a New Construct

Our current reality of church—in the shape of a pyramid with power and resources often going up—is a construct. The patterns of patriarchy and hierarchy have been constructed by following patterns of empire, made worse by capitalistic and consumeristic values. We forget that we are free to choose, to imagine and create, another way. Another way is possible! The question becomes, what could it look like to follow Jesus in co-creating another way?

Surely you know this constructed reality and the harm it has caused countless people, as well as the earth, is still a far cry from our potential as humanity, even when considering the immense joy and love that has been passed down through generations. Can we imagine a future church supported on all levels by values of compassion, gentleness, love, balance, justice, and kindness without the harm? Can we imagine a future church where the faith, insights, experiences, and wisdom from women are honored equally? Moreover, can we imagine a future church where the perspectives and wisdom from people outside of the church (many of whom were harmed, minimized, or otherwise not welcomed) are honored? Can we imagine that it is possible to align ourselves with the energy of Divine Love that is moving in the world? Can we believe that God is doing *a new thing* (Isaiah 43:19) and can we open ourselves up to the possibility that Divine Love is doing a new thing *through us*? Can our faith be big enough to believe that another paradigm is not only possible, but that God can work through everyday people like you and me to co-create it?

Mary, the Divine Mother of Jesus who embodies the Sacred Feminine, showed us how to have strong faith in a future that is still unseen. She had so much faith in her son, Jesus, that she sang a song praising Jesus' actions as though he had *already* changed the world, even though she was still pregnant with him! Before his feet ever touched the earth, she was giving thanks for all the good that he would do.

> *And Mary said, "My soul magnifies the Lord, and my spirit rejoices in God my Savior, for he has looked with favor on the lowliness of his servant...He has shown strength with his arm; he has scattered the proud in the thoughts of their hearts. He has brought down the powerful from their thrones and lifted up the lowly; he has filled the hungry with good things and sent the rich away empty."*
>
> —LUKE 1:46–48, 51–53

Not only could Mary's words be a key to what future church looks like, as the powerful are brought down and the humble are lifted up, but she reminds us that we too can have strong faith in a future we cannot yet see. Shifting our language and our vision to proclaim that the future is here, now, is not only a key to co-creation, it is a Christian concept, firmly rooted in the Divine Feminine spirit of Mary. Mary models a posture of belief that is so strong that she is already praising and giving thanks for that which will come to pass in the future.

With the faith of Mary, I write about future church as though it has already happened, because I know that the spiritual advancement of humanity is inevitable and that followers of Jesus are and will continue to be a part of it.

I can see the ways that the seeds of Christ consciousness, divine rhema, and the divine feminine have now yielded beautiful fields of flowers. We have co-created this new reality, together. Join me in envisioning and co-creating the church as I believe it will be in the future.

PART 1: RECLAIM, RESTORE, AND RENEW

It's been said that every 500 years or so, the Church goes through a great upheaval—a revolution of sorts. Phyllis Tickle, in *The Great Emergence: How Christianity is Changing and Why*, points to this grand theory by reminding us that the Great Reformation took place 500 years ago. The Great Schism (the split between the Eastern and Western Church) was 500 years before that, and Pope Gregory the Great helped to bring the church out of the Dark Ages before that. We have established these cycles and patterns as part of nature, of society, and of history. I have every reason to believe and celebrate Phyllis Tickle's wisdom, and I also am aware that Indigenous cultures have long rested on the understanding of great cycles of nature and history. We are, once again, on the cusp of another great cycle, another turn in the spiral toward the spiritual advancement of humanity.

I consider this time to be the Great Renewal. The currents of deconstructing church and the conversations and movements toward decolonization have allowed us to, on a macro level, peel away that which is no longer serving the body of Christ. More than peeling away, they have become compost—fertile ground, from which new ways of being church are already emerging. The releasing of what has caused harm is a massive exhale that is, in many ways, still taking place. We are still exhaling and letting go of that which no longer furthers our spiritual growth in Love. And yet, after this great exhale, we collectively have space to allow in that which was suppressed and rejected by patriarchy and church-as-empire—namely, an ever-deeper awareness of emotion, intuition, heart, balance and integration, and compassion for self, others, and the world. This "allowing in" results in a "great renewal" of our faith. In this moment, there is a contrast between that which no longer serves a spirit of Divine Love and that which we hope and long for. In this energetic field of contrast, we have space to imagine and allow in potentials for the future church that we desire.

Reclaiming Jesus' Three Levels of Love

We as a people of God (the "church" is now *all* of us who seek to follow Christ, not just members of churches with buildings) proclaim and bless the beauty of the exchange of Love on an individual level, on a community level, and a worldly level, mirroring Jesus' prayer in John 17, and mirroring the way Jesus impacted those around him. We are inspired by the notion that Divine Love (God) spirals outward and goes far beyond the church building. The love of God is expansive and includes ALL the ways we exchange love, from helping a child bake banana bread for an elderly neighbor, to making love, to preparing dinner for friends and family, tutoring, delivering a meal, visiting someone who is lonely, protesting, playing games, as well as festivals and school activities. Love of partners, being there for one another in sickness and in health, that ongoing I'm-with-you-through-thick-and-thin love. All this is part of Divine Love. What does loving your neighbors—those who live closely around you—look like? What about loving our neighbors who live across the railroad tracks? How can our love for community spiral out to impact the world? All of this is God's love.

Future church has reclaimed an expansive understanding of how we participate in the reign of Love in the world around us, and it starts with relationships and interconnection. Gone are the days of "outreach ministries" that were devoid of relationship and functioned in a top-down capacity, meaning that the church decided how they served others who had no say in the matter, with no desire to know the individuals they are serving. Gone are the days where the ministry of the "church" was kept primarily in the church building and only for church members. Gone are the days where committees, programs, and paid staff determined what following Jesus looked like for others. Like Jesus, we spiral out, with an ever-expanding concept of love. When we see this with Christ eyes, then we see that a church committee or leadership position in the church is not a better way to serve God than a teen raking leaves for an elderly neighbor. Indeed, that which is carried out in a spirit of love is more connected to God, regardless of church clothing and vestments, titles, or whether the act of love takes place in or around a church building. Divine Love reverberates through all the earth, so any exchange of Love is a dance with God.

Restoring Wholeness, Liberation from Shame

We now see that it benefitted the old way of being church to perpetuate shame and a fear of damnation and judgement. Believers flocked to church, leaning on clergy to determine when they were right in the eyes of God. Meanwhile, the shadow side of people were pushed down and made unconscious. Not eliminated, mind you, just not recognized and brought to the light. The corruption, harm, and abuse we have seen in churches against women, people of color, LGBTQ people, and children became evidence that the church was not actually any holier or more whole than the rest of the world. It became evidence that their own shadow side needed to be exposed.

When we began to integrate the Divine Feminine, it allowed us to begin recovering our shadow sides—the parts of ourselves that have been rejected by the church and society. This was how we liberated ourselves from shame and restored wholeness to our lives. This holistic shift moves us toward Christ consciousness—a mystic understanding of Christ in us, around us, and a part of all of creation. The result: we began experiencing an expansion of what we consider to be sacred.

Liberated from shame, we now look at ourselves wholly and deeply. We can examine the wounds caused by generations prior, by other people, and even ourselves. We are safe to see them, love ourselves, and forgive ourselves and others. All of who we are is loved by God. We are wholly loved, even our wounds, cracks, and scars. By forgiving ourselves and having compassion for ourselves first, it allows us to have compassion and forgiveness toward others. In Genesis, everything that God created, God said was good. God blessed it all. It was in this blessing, in this goodness, that we transformed our shadows, the hidden parts of ourselves, into the light. Therefore, shame and judgement have no power over us anymore. This was liberating to us and perplexing to churches that still used shame and judgement to convince people to go to church.

Reclaiming Joy

Once control and shame had no power over us anymore, we began to love ourselves, one another, our communities, and the world through a spirit of joy, rather than duty and guilt. In the past, a spirit of duty was honorable in many ways. But in other ways, duty meant doing what some people considered the "right thing" in a joyless frame of mind. Now, we experience the abundant joy that Jesus promised us in this expanded way of being church as well as by seeing the world through Christ's eyes. Christ consciousness allows us to enjoy a spirit of light-heartedness, laughter, delight, and surprise in our life. We no longer label enjoyable activities as hedonistic. Enjoying the beach or the lake is communing with God's creation. Playing with a child is loving and receiving God's love from another person—this is sacred! A delicious meal allows us to acknowledge abundance and provision. Dancing, reading, feeding others, comedy, sex, learning, healing prayers, hiking, eating, cleaning, working, teaching—all of these things can be done in a spirit of joy, seeing each one as part of the Divine Love in all things and all people. Living life conscious of Christ—of love!—in every part of life is a joy.

Restoring a Spirit of Curiosity and Wonder

Reclaiming silence allowed us to deeply perceive how Divine Love moves in our lives, in the lives of our loved ones, and in the natural world. And once we noticed that, we began to restore the spirit of curiosity and wonder that we had as children. We began to experience the wild through the eyes of a child. We experience synchronicities as signs of alignment with Divine Love in the world. In the silence of our communal gatherings, which centered belonging, not membership, we made space to share our moments of wonder and awe, allowing us to, once again, see the grandeur of life and God, and to see ourselves as co-creators with divine potential and promise. Seeds of hope grew from the apathy we sent to the compost pile. Seeds of wonder grew when we liberated ourselves from dogma that once stifled and controlled us. At some point, we noticed the power of healing that was happening amongst us. We experienced healing from generations of colonization and war. We began to heal from loved ones that hurt us, unintentionally or not. We began to heal from the messages from our childhood that we were "too *this*" or "not enough of *that*." Once we learned to perceive Divine Love in the world, we could sense the potential for us to co-create our healing and our renewed sense of seeing the world through the eyes of a child.

Reclaiming Sexuality as a Gift

We are finally purged from the remnants of the puritanical idea of sexuality as a sin, an embarrassment, and something to hide and be shameful of. Church avoided the topic of sex so much that they created a huge shadow that only served to harm primarily women, LGBTQ people, and children in secret. We now are comfortable embracing the goodness of sexuality. It is, after all, how we create other humans, how we show love, how we play, and how we enjoy one another in a spirit of love. Of course, like other things, it can be misused and abused, especially when church used to have a distorted way of dealing with the topic. Now that we see sexuality as part of the creation that is of God, we can bring it to the light and reclaim it as good and joyful.

A Renewed Emphasis on Financial Transparency

> "The point is this: the one who sows sparingly will also reap sparingly, and the one who sows bountifully will also reap bountifully. Each of you must give as you have made up your mind, not reluctantly or under compulsion, for God loves a cheerful giver. And God is able to provide you with every blessing in abundance, so that by always having enough of everything, you may share abundantly in every good work."
> —2 CORINTHIANS 9:6–8

A distinct difference with future church is that many faith communities and churches disentangled ourselves from excess profit-making. Too much focus on money and protecting money was wrapped up into being the body of Christ from institutional churches that made seemingly good organizations act like church-as-empire. Their level of protection of assets meant that money was given priority over caring for people who were being harmed or in a place of vulnerability. Couple that with the model of hierarchy and we saw the church-as-empire's money going up and staying within the church, rather than leaving the institution and directly benefitting those most in need. A lack of transparency was such a part of the system of church-as-empire that congregants willingly gave money without fully understanding how little was directly going to causes that mirror the way that Jesus lived. Millions were spent on liability issues, grand ordinations, church events, and church properties that were underutilized six days of the week. Many who are now part of the future church were eager to liberate ourselves from money-making and layers of spiritual authority. We created a culture of church that empowers individuals and circles to decide how their financial resources and the gift of their time should directly impact and bless the community and the world. This, admittedly, looks quite different than the ways of the past. Our version of church doesn't have paid staff or buildings. We combine our giving to decide by consensus how it will impact the community. We lead through facilitation and listening, and we are all empowered to be active to the ability that we can. There are no paid professionals for many future churches now. Those of us who embody church in this way believe this to be more in alignment with Jesus' teachings. These changes took time and there was upheaval. Imagine the uncomfortable turbulence of individuals sharing stories of harm in the church that were once silenced, the shock from church members, and the conflict that arises when churches that are resistant to have their shadow sides revealed are demanded to be transparent and face justice. Church leaders rose up to share the abuse from other church leaders. The upheaval was uncomfortable, but necessary. It took time, but we actually shifted the culture of the wider church for the better. Even traditional examples of church now are more transparent with finances, which puts pressure on churches as they are held accountable for ensuring that financial resources are aligned with Christ's values for humanity and the world. Non-disclosure agreements within the church are now a thing of the past, where they should stay. Enabling church leaders who abuse others is no longer tolerated. It took a large number of us speaking up, speaking out and shining a light on practices and patterns that not only didn't serve the greater good but caused harm toward others. Now, transparency of organizations and churches is the norm.

Reclaiming the Power of Forgiveness and Reparations

For all the attention that churches have given to forgiving and to confessing our sins, it was challenging for those of us who were harmed to work on a process of forgiving the church (including the church leaders) that harmed us. The process of forgiving felt ongoing. We thought we were done, but lingering resentment and anger showed us that we had more forgiveness to do. We reclaimed the liberating power of forgiveness for ourselves. We too are part of future church.

And many churches and religious institutions, to their credit, took on the process of reconciliation and exploring reparations toward those of us who have been harmed.

The first step for reparations was not uttering words of repentance. We weren't interested in empty words. The first step was, as Jesus says, becoming like a child. The church has learned to walk again in new ways. It has learned to be the church in new ways.

The church has learned to depend on a Father / Mother God who is greater than it is. The church learned to become a community of Christ followers with integrity and honesty and approached this endeavor of learning to be the church in new ways with the heart of a child, who learns to walk by falling multiple times, yet gets back up again. Church leaders now are openly aware of the tendencies of institutional church and denominations to put the business of the church before the teachings of Christ. To counteract this human tendency, they have elevated leaders who have modeled the posture of a child with a pure heart, dependent on God.

Restoring a Spirit of Gentleness After a History of Force

After 2000 years of colonizing Christianity telling cultures and people how to think and what to believe, and threatening with fear, violence, or shame, people are waking up to the fact that they don't want to be forced into their beliefs. So how do we as people of faith counteract that? We do it with listening. We do it by adopting a spirit of gentleness and listening. Gentle is the way. We listen to how the Spirit is leading now, rather than dictating it for other people. We listen and we yield, and we observe and reflect that Spirit is already moving in people's lives. We cultivate a greater ability to perceive Divine Love, and we encourage one another to listen for the Spirit themselves. We invite people to be a part of our faith circles, faith communities, and churches, with a spirit of gentleness and sincerity. Coercion is a thing of the past.

PART 2: FROM INWARD TO OUTWARD

A New Understanding Of An Ancient Cycle: Spirals Expand Out

Many church leaders often speak of the rhythm of in and out; it's part of church culture. It has been said that we go in the church building for worship, singing, fellowship, study of Scripture, and then we leave, nourished, to go out in the world. This is similar to our rhythm of breath and the cycle of the moon waxing and waning; it is a cycle of nature and life. However, with future church, we wanted to move toward a more faithful embodiment of the life of Christ, so we now value regularly drawing inward in quiet to commune with God. In fact, coming into the doors of a church is optional. Drawing inward in quiet to connect with your spirit—with the "*Christ that abides in you*" and the "*still small voice*" of the heart—is essential for us.

Following Jesus Beyond Church Walls

> *"Do you not know that your body is a temple of the Holy Spirit within you, which you have from God, and that you are not your own?"*
> —1 CORINTHIANS 6:19

The depth to which we turn inward mirrors the breadth to which we practice loving compassion in the world around us. With church-as-empire, which is falling away, a shallow breath in was leading to a shallow breath out. The impact of shallow cycles impacted the health of the church just as shallow breathing impacts the health of people. There were little to no moments of silence in worship; little to no cultivation of listening to our rhema—what God was saying to us in the still of our hearts. Meanwhile, its shallow breath out meant that the energy, income, and ministries of a church often stayed in, or went up in the levels of hierarchy, even as there was a shallow expression of hands-on service that impacted lives in the community around them, in the spirit of Jesus.

In this ancient cycle of in and out like the breath, the pattern of Jesus' life was to turn away at times to pray in silence, reconnecting with God before many pivotal moments in his life. Before choosing the twelve disciples, before the well-known miracle of Jesus leaving his boat to walk on water amidst strong winds, and before the miracle of five loaves and two fish, Jesus withdrew from people to go to a deserted place to pray. Jesus, whose care and compassion for others is unparalleled, was spiritually fed by turning inward to God in prayer. Meanwhile, with church-as-empire, we mirrored the culture of programs, capitalism, loudness, and outward authority. Why would an older expression of church want to cultivate our ability to listen to our spirits when they counted attendance for who listened to sermons from a pulpit and considered that number to be a sign of success?

Future church follows the spirit of Jesus, who modeled another way. The difference in the inward movement is not about being inside the doors of the church. It's inside of *you*. It's not in and out of a building, it's in the heart, in our very being. In the spirit and then out in the community. When we draw within—in our spirit, versus in the building, the depth to which we can go outward is magnified exponentially. This inevitably leads to a greater ability to use our buildings for the wider community. When we acknowledge that Christ abides in us and Christ abides in others, we can begin to co-create in a spirit of collaboration and mutual blessing.[41] In this way, future church has, finally, liberated our divinity and allows us to follow Jesus beyond church walls.

For the new expression of community circles (church), that means that we often honor a period of time for silence when we gather together, in addition to prioritizing silence on a daily basis individually. We take time to listen to how the Spirit is moving in the silence of our lives. We notice synchronicities, signs, and the quiet voice from within. In traditional churches (with buildings), many now offer teachings and guidance in listening to our divine rhema. People who have cultivated the ability to listen to divine rhema and exude wisdom, humility, and love are often elevated to leadership positions for those faith communities that have a hierarchical model. There are now times of silence in worship services—not just a few seconds, but real silence. And it has become common for Christians to meditate, practice contemplative prayer, or other methods of experiencing God within us. This allows us to remain rooted to God and in a state of balance, despite the storms of life.

This cultural shift has also encouraged a deeper level of compassion and understanding. We are more secure in our relationship and experience of God because we finally live into the deep knowledge of the Christ that abides within. The Great Renewal is well underway.

PART 3: WELCOMING THE SPIRIT

We have liberated the meaning of "church." It is no longer exclusively tied to a church building, membership, or a denomination. A more expansive understanding of church began to rise up alongside the more traditional understanding, so now people have more options. Church now means two or more people gathering who acknowledge the spirit of Christ that is present everywhere, including with them. We needed new models of leadership outside of hierarchy. Hierarchy presupposes that the higher people at the top, those who have been given more authority, are closer to God. But that is not accurate. For some of us, our grandparents and ancestors are great examples of people who were close to God but without authority in a church. Anyone can draw near to God. God does not have preferences in order or titles.

With this newer understanding of church, authority figures are not required for church anymore, because we individually know how to listen to our spirits. We know what it takes to draw near to God. Furthermore, not only does the size of our gatherings not matter anymore, smaller is usually preferred, so that we can listen and learn from one another's rhema, the wisdom revealed by God to us individually. In a smaller setting, we know others and are known. Our gatherings are authentic, warm, meaningful, and joyful. Buildings are also optional. We can gather anywhere, from people's homes, on nature trails, in picnic shelters, coffee shops, community centers—anywhere we want to gather.

Our gatherings are circular and mutual. No one has more authority or power. There are often one or two guardians of a circle (church) who act as facilitators, ensuring that a spirit of love and the honoring of each person takes place. These circles can also be considered house churches or neighborhood churches. And each circle determines how they will be a presence of love in their communities. They do this by listening to the wisdom of their community and how God is moving in their hopes, longings, and dreams, rather than assuming they know how to best meet other people's needs. We listen for the gifts and wisdom in others and partner with our community to be a blessing within the community. Compassionate action is done *with* and *among* others, not *to* them or *for* them. The days of "outreach" removed from relationship that used to be more common with brick and mortar churches are fading away. Circle churches embody and become love in their community in countless humble ways and bigger is not always better. Playing music for children, helping out with chores for the elderly, providing meals for people with food insecurity, tending community gardens, or providing homework help for children are just a few. Circle churches often partner together in collaboration with other circle churches, non-profits, and people to meet the needs of the wider community. We model a circular, expanding pattern that spirals out to our communities and neighborhoods, rather than a hierarchical model. We have created intricate networks of compassionate action, which emerged once we began understanding our interconnectedness to a greater degree. Now, church isn't anthropocentric like church-as-empire was. We are interconnected to earth, and we understand the natural world to be conscious and alive, full of Divine Love as we are. We seek to be guardians of our sacred land, God's first sanctuary. We give back, honor, and respect the dignity of Earth and animals.

In many ways, what has happened is nothing short of a revolution of the heart, on an individual level and a collective level. Many of us gave up needing to see faith leaders in church robes, needing to be in grand church buildings, and needing to use an excess of titles and honorifics, which often perpetuated a hierarchy of importance and fed egos. There is no longer a climb to the top of a hierarchical model, but rather the circular shape where love spirals around the circle and out in our communities. Our circular, mutual model is rooted in humility and servanthood, not power and authority. Our guardians of the faith do not have salaries or titles; they serve with a pure intention of guarding (but not controlling) how we live out our faith in our faith community.

Many of us came from traditional churches that had all sorts of trainings. Churches that perpetuated harm were often up to date in the mandated and well-meaning trainings for a safe church. Trainings might seek to change your mind, but the traditional church needed a change of heart, a change of how they operated as a system. We found that the traditional church needed a shift in values so that the values of Jesus are always front and center, regardless of whether that is the most profitable outcome for a church. Christianity must be centered on values of the heart, values of compassion. That should be how we measure our success. As Mother Teresa said, "God has not called us to be successful, only that we be faithful." Our Christ eyes show us that being faithful *is* being successful. Success is not the path that always results in financial profit, and church culture is now clear with that. Our circles allowed us to experience the revolution of the heart that our spirits were longing for. Ironically, the industrial revolution meant that items such as textiles and tools made in the home became made outside of the home, on machines, driving the goals of profitability. This revolution of the heart brings our faith community back to the home and to the local community, as we seek space from the profit, power, and control of church-as-empire. If our revolution had a theme song, it would be Mary's Magnificat, for each circle chooses to be free from the all-powerful as we align ourselves with a humble movement rooted in love.

Our "success," if we use that term, is found in our faithfulness, not in numbers. Is the local church faithful in the ways we serve and love our neighbors and community? Are we faithful in our desire to be the love of Christ in the world and in our homes? Are we faithful in our ability to love and care for ourselves, honoring the sabbath and seeking balanced lives? Are we kind, just, humble, and merciful? And are we living lives of abundant joy in the spirit of Christ? We decide what faithfulness looks like for us.

Love of Neighbor Is Greater than Conversion.

Our desire to "be love" in the world is greater than our desire to convert, and, ironically, we realized by embodying love in the world, we naturally draw people to the path of Jesus far more than coercive efforts to instill fear, shame, or control ever did. Love is our creed. Love is our mission. Love is our value. Not fear, judgement, shame, control, or numbers. Not budgets, professional music, programs, or hierarchy. Jesus never modeled that anyway. Now we can see the difference between a patriarchal construct and the simple words of Jesus. Love is breaking bread together, blessing others with a word of grace and encouragement, a warm hug for the lonely, justice for those in poverty, and a healing prayer for the sick. Love treats all people, including women, with the same honor and respect.

Love is seeking to find and include the least, the lost, the last, and the looked over. Love is aligning ourselves in a spirit of solidarity with anyone who has been harmed, abused, hurt, or is in a state of sorrow. Love is a joy, not a duty, and it begins with loving ourselves! We allow God's love to begin in our heart and we allow ourselves to receive love. Then, that love overflows to the love of our families and friends, our households, our neighbors, our communities, and the world. To become the future church, we sought a balance to the history of patriarchy by embodying the Divine Feminine values of compassion, internal authority, and Christ consciousness—the awareness of Christ in all things, and a return to honoring the divine in the natural world. We co-create a new paradigm every time we are conscious enough to listen to God speaking to our spirit—we are guided every step of the way. There is no need to manipulate or control others in order to invite people into the love of our faith. Love begets love.

Ultimate Purpose and Power of Community

You may be asking, "What is the purpose of this expanded understanding of church, if God is everywhere, including inside all of us? What's the purpose of all of us gathering together at all if we are to connect with God within?" Well, the purpose is community. Community is still incredibly important. But, when we connect with God within and when we flow with the synchronicity of what God is doing in the world, then, when the community gathers together in the name of Jesus Christ, we are able to BE Christ in the world in a more profound, meaningful, and impactful way because we are conscious of the power of Christ within us and others. In many cases a church building is still a gathering spot, a place to gather for worship and renewal. But the work of the church—how we follow Jesus—is done in the world. Most of us still find meaning in gathering to sing, pray, and worship in ways that are deeply meaningful and contextual! But we are now fully conscious of the notion that God is within us and others. This awareness heightens the sacredness of our rituals and worship. It heightens the sacredness of our conversations with neighbors and our service in our community. We don't only connect with God in worship now. We have spiritually expanded to understand that we connect with God in others and in the world too because there is nowhere God is not present. We now know that engaging our community in a spirit of God's love is key to nurturing thriving communities and thriving churches/faith circles. There is an easy and effortless flow of going within as individuals to listen to God, gathering as followers of Jesus to listen to one another's wisdom, sing, pray, and be together, and serving the world around us in a spirit of joy and compassion.

For a growing number of us, our smaller circles allow us to more easily follow the way of Jesus. We share our abundance, our gifts, and our resources with our communities directly, as Jesus would do, rather than send our resources up to the higher ranks for a church to distribute it for us, without our input or knowledge of where it goes. After all, Mary sings that the lowly have been lifted up and the high have been brought down! We like to stay low, in the grassroots of our community, strengthening, empowering, and being among those most in need. We have taken back our power and our ability to form communities, gather together, and acknowledge that our divinity is within us, rather than outside of us. We gather where we want to, when we want to. We gather in gardens to share food. We gather in homes over a meal. We gather in coffee shops.

We gather at local non-profits to engage in compassionate action. We understand that every time we have a meal, Jesus is known to us. We pray with words and without words. Our listening to God is our prayer.

We deeply understand that we are able to be healing agents—repairers of the breach. And there is always healing that needs to happen. Individuals need healing from emotional or physical harm, and collectively our world needs healing. Our grassroots churches/faith circles promote healing and reconciliation with the millions of people who had to leave their churches for their well-being. We seek to open our homes and hearts to accept and love people who seek to journey with us. We hope that God's love and kindness, shown by our actions and words, will over time become balms for wounded and weary souls. There is healing that needs to happen between neighbors and family members over political divides, racism, classism, misogyny, prejudice over people who love differently and look different. There is healing that needs to dissolve the tension between nations and ethnicities. One home, one heart, one conversation at a time, we seek to embody the healing love of Christ, who we believe can work miracles during times of tension and upheaval.

We value transparency over secrecy, grassroots community over hierarchy, and there are no higher ranks, for we are all children of God. Because our circles are small, we really know one another. We value authenticity and vulnerability. Our shadow sides are not only allowed to be named, they are known and loved as we bring it to the light. We don't hide our woundedness from one another.

We accompany one another in following Jesus beyond the old version of church's walls, to a greater understanding of divinity within. We deeply value collaboration, whether with other circle churches, traditional churches, or other people to serve our communities and bless our communities and other regions of the world in need. We take time to listen to our visions and hopes, and we even practice co-creating our visions together. We take time to vision, individually and communally, and we consider this to be a multi-dimensional form of praying that utilizes our inner sight, our emotions, our energy, our mind, and our faith. If we envision a community with no hunger, then we agree upon our intentions and begin to have conversations and collaborations to work toward a common goal that there is abundant food for all. It is a joy to co-create the reign of Love around us!

We also value freedom over control. We decide the music we want to hear. We decide whether there is a need to confess or repent, or praise and give thanks. We lead our own prayers. Our church, humble as it is, honors the spirit of Jesus in beautiful ways. We empower one another to be the love of Christ in community rather than to hold power within a church structure, up its ranks, and within its authority. Our collected offerings often go directly to those in need in the community, and we often give significantly since we choose not to hire staff or own our own church buildings and property.

As simple as it sounds, we have recovered the original intent of humanity, which is to be deeply connected in mutuality, respect, awe, and love of nature, one another, and God.

Expanding Church Means More Options, not "One or the Other"

Some churches have church buildings and are an important part of future church. The churches that own buildings and property and embody faithfulness have often made some important cultural shifts in order to be as viable as circle churches and are growing and thriving. These churches strive to make a significant impact in their local community in decolonized ways, supporting relational engagement. They are incredibly transparent with their funds and have lean staff, choosing to prioritize resources going to the local community. One easy way to tell if a church with a building is faithful in their community impact is that whenever you drive by one during the week or on the weekend, the parking lot is often full because they have partnered with community organizations or are directly serving the needs of the community within their building. The rooms, buildings, and property are being utilized for purposes outside of Sunday worship or even church ministries. These churches emphasize love, lifting up the lowly, justice work, care for the earth, healing, reconciliation, feeding, and collaboration. They strive to be a hub for people and organizations to better their community. They no longer use tactics of shame, fear, or control because there has been a culture shift—people would not support a church that wants them to feel unworthy of God's abundant love and the power of God within us. These churches open their doors wide open to people who experience homelessness, addiction, hunger, loneliness, or illness. They also understand that "church" means being the love of God in the community, not just within their buildings. They tend to do a great job with discipleship—sending followers of Jesus out in the community. This is supported by a strong emphasis on contemplative practices that allow individuals and the church community to listen to their divine rhema and be conscious of our "little Christ" that abides within each of us. Our cups are filled by God's love found in the quiet, as well as larger gathered worship. In all of these practices, the church community openly communicates their sincere desire to welcome the wider community's participation. Folks outside of church used to feel like they were "othered" by church members because they were not active members of a church, but that feeling has subsided and we all mutually acknowledge and respect these varied ways of gathering as church and faith communities.

 Now, people can choose lively preaching rooted in love and moving music from a church with a building, or conversation and good news from a circle of people, also with music that they choose. And some people choose both. We have more options now, and the steady increase of circle churches means that churches with buildings are more accountable to the higher, more noble values that came about when we walked away from hierarchical models that denied their need for reform. The process to get here wasn't always easy, but the result has benefitted everyone.

Looking at the Present, with the Wisdom of the Future

You've seen a vision of future church. So what does that mean for you, in the *present-now*?

If worship leaves you spiritually fed, filled with joy, and if you heard and experienced the Good News of Christ, and if there is a regular movement to take the teachings of Jesus into community in a spirit of love, then rejoice and give thanks. God can absolutely be honored and glorified in the church and outside of the church. And there are plenty of good churches and good church leaders. I know hundreds of them. I actually have great love for the intentions held by the vast majority of people associated with our churches. Loving relationships, sincere prayers and worship, and countless examples of service to others are taking place in and around community-oriented churches. The reality, also, is this: the vast majority of churches spend a small percentage of their budget on the concerns of those who suffer in their community. The vast majority of finances support buildings, property, salaries, utilities, and church programming (which primarily benefits the members). Some churches also give a percentage that goes up—to regional, state, or nationwide structures of the church. Then, after "the church" is taken care of, a very small percentage goes to the very people Jesus cared most about. The structure is such that most of the time and energy is also spent supporting the church inside of the church building, rather than out, in the community. And this says nothing of the shadow side of Christianity, where misogyny is a strong and steady current moving just under the surface, bubbling up more and more.

The churches with buildings that are doing well in the *future-now* came face-to-face with the shadow side of Christianity in a spirit of love and compassion for the wounded. In a variety of ways, they took seriously the harm caused to women through harassment, misogyny, and shame. They faced a public reckoning, not only with women, but children, people of color, LGBTQ people, and countless ancestors. The process of reckoning and reconciliation is still ongoing, but these churches didn't deny there was a problem. Their spiritual maturity and humility has allowed them to continue to this day. They showed that they cared for the lowly, even when the lowly were the voices crying out against the unchecked power of the church.

Many of them also collaborate with church circles—the many smaller groups found throughout communities. Now, we have come to a place where we fully respect the type of church that people choose, whether it's various denominations, churches with buildings, or circle churches. People have the freedom to choose the type of church that meets their needs, and we all work together to be the reign of Love in our homes, in our communities, and in the world. And everyone understands why a big percentage of followers of Jesus don't want to be in a church building again. They understand with compassion, not judgement. And now, they can be a part of a circle church anywhere, if they want. In the spirit of God's love, we seek to improve lives and our earth with fellow Christians, with believers of other faiths and religions, and with agnostics and atheists. We are, finally, becoming united in a spirit of love and compassion and we respect the variety of beliefs and faiths as we collaborate toward a better world for us all.

Even though churches with buildings still exist, for a growing number of us, there is less interest in the old way of "going" to church. The church is us, the people! *We* are the church. Wherever two or three of us are gathered, Christ is in the midst of us. We no longer need a church building to remind us of the significance of community when we can gather anywhere, at any time. The church is the *people*, not a building. And denominations and churches with buildings and staff are no longer the only way to live into the power of a faith community. We have expanded our understanding of church. We took back our power because the way the Spirit moves goes far beyond the boxes of patriarchal and hierarchical understandings of church. Many of us who are now part of circle churches came from a church that did not seek to offer healing or reconciliation for their acts of harm and did not acknowledge a history of perpetuating acts of oppression and injustice in the name of God. Others of us simply prefer this way. We like the freedom, the smaller, authentic community, and the spiritual expansion. We like listening to one another's divine rhema, practicing our Christ consciousness, and integrating our concept of the Divine Mother with the Divine Father. We like the joy! Every day, circles are being started and are growing. This is future church. We can choose to become and step into the future, now.

You may be wondering about how folks outside of traditional church see and understand resurrection. It's varied, of course. The beauty of the resurrection is that it can be seen everywhere. It is not meant to be only talked about within the walls of the church. The resurrection can be seen through every daffodil that comes back again in the spring. It can be seen through every tree that goes through the process of losing leaves in the barrenness of winter and then grows fresh, new, green leaves each year. Yet the most beautiful example, for many of us, is witnessing new life and resurrection in individuals—witnessing what looks like death, and then rebirth, and resurrection. It's a messy process, not unlike the process that the culture of church is undergoing. An example of people who showcase resurrection so beautifully are those who have been in the grip of addiction and then end up clean and sober. It is a rough journey and a close look at this process reveals it to be anything but beautiful. This journey is raw and requires surrender and honesty. It's similar to a caterpillar going through the process of unbecoming in its cocoon and eventually transforming to a butterfly. The end result is beautiful. We don't need to go to church on Sundays to understand resurrection.

To see resurrection, we look to the people we know who have been on their knees in death and in sorrow and then have gone through the process of re-birth and living a new life. We look in the mirror. We look at church. We know that this possibility of resurrection is there for each and every one of us.

Jesus' death and resurrection is reflected in trees, flowers, and us too. And yes, we still tell the story of Jesus' life and Jesus' resurrection. We are also witnesses to Jesus' death and resurrection because Christ abides in us, too. We, who are the future church, are experiencing the fruits of renewal and resurrection of the church of the past! We experience the eternal life and the endless cycles (spirals) of growth of we who are the body of Christ. From the future, we stretch out our hands to you as we sing our Alleluias! Join us on the journey toward resurrection and renewal.

Reflection Questions: Chapter 9

- What hope or claim can you make about future church in the future tense with the faith of Mary?
- How could a *Great Renewal* tangibly impact your life?
- What is a practical first step toward future church in your context? For example, if you are a member of a church, what action steps can you take to promote increased transparency of finances and communication at your church?
- If you are a part of a faith community, do you believe ample resources and time are going outward, to impact the needs in your community? If not, what can you do about that?
- How could the concept of the inward-outward movement of church being within you (rather than inside the church building) and then moving out into community potentially revolutionize our understanding of church and God?
- In what ways can you be a healing agent in your local context in the spirit of Christ's love?

10

Awaken and Rise, Guardians of the Faith!

AWAKEN TO TIME AS A SPIRAL

We have been taught to understand time as linear, but I have repeatedly experienced that an integral part of life growth and expanding spiritually is to open our mind to the notion of time as a spiral. Certain themes or life lessons circle back around every few years, giving us choices as to the role we will play. Once we understand that themes of our life will spiral back around, we can choose to act based on what we have learned before. In several ways, I can see how time spirals and life lessons spiral back around. The energy of parts of my life circles back to me and gives me choices, and each time I can grow and spiritually expand in that theme. I can see the themes in my own life of being harmed, being judged when I meekly spoke up, and striving to fit in when I was meant to not fit in. But now as time circles back around, I stand tall as I speak up with a stronger voice, calling other sisters and people of faith to stand with me, and I am at peace with being on the margins of church. More than at peace, I stand here with pride, inviting others to this holy place, for God is here, too.

Christ consciousness gives us the eyes to see that time is not only linear, but also a spiral. By being present and aware in the here and now, we can notice the way that God has moved and is moving in our lives. So whether I sit in silence or go on a walk, which is meditating to me, then I am uncoupling the spirit from the mind, and it is my spirit that guides me towards these spiritual lessons that are spiraling back around.

It's beautiful to notice the spiraling pattern, which often presents itself in years. Ten years ago, I felt like putrid compost as I was in the most painful time of my life, experiencing the trauma of sexual harassment, the church trial, and rejection from my church. During the midst of this painful time, I remember wondering where I would be ten years later. It gave me a measure of hope to imagine I would not always be in such pain. And here I am, writing this to you. God has healed my wounds, guided me to walk with churches and grassroots circles so they can be the love of Christ in their communities, and given me the strength to share my story in hopes that we can better our faith. Look how God moves! Look how time is a spiral. I thought I would never share this story. Sharing about what happened to me in high school did not end well. It also didn't end well when I reported my supervisor in the church. But after I shared what had happened to me at the women's conference and other women started coming to me, I saw I was not alone. And I remember that still small voice, "When you stand up for justice, the world will rise to meet you." So here I am, ten years later, writing these vulnerable words in hopes that you will rise to join me in this moment. Perhaps time is a spiral for you too.

A Pattern of the Universe

One common pattern of nature and the universe is the spiral fractal. Each year trees go through repeating cycles of quiet winters with bare leaves, to tender green leaves, to the fullness of summer leaves, and then the changing colors of fall. And each year they grow outward, their branches reaching toward the light. This is the way of nature. This is also the way that time unfolds.

We spiral through patterns of intense creativity and momentum, patterns of waiting and receiving what we have intended and worked toward, cycles of work and rest, co-creation and play. Time waxes and wanes, circles and spirals. A linear concept of time is man-made rather than inspired from creation. Since a fractal is a never-ending pattern and is found throughout the world, it makes sense that our concept of time can also be perceived as circling or spiraling back round.

And if time can spiral back around, then so too can what we learn from history and how this applies to our spiritual growth. It's time that we go back and reclaim that which we have buried or forgotten from the very beginning of our faith. This shadow work is key to our expansion. We can reclaim the very concept of God, or Divine Love, that we are rooted to.

The pattern of churches right now is linear in time and does not value spiritual expansion in the same way. There are many who don't desire to reflect on the buried shadow side of our faith, even though it is circling back around again through the movement of deconstruction and the rise of spirituality. And across the history of time, an assimilation of industrial values or capitalistic values has meant that the language of nature has fallen out of our modern dialect. The culture, values, and ways of our Indigenous ancestors have been suppressed over hundreds of years. It's time that we reflect on what we have considered progress and success in both society and the church, being open to the notion that we can make new decisions, now. Over time we have come to rely less on nature as sanctuary. We have forgotten that Mother Earth is capable of having her own wisdom in her own language. Christ consciousness and the integration of the Divine Feminine can give us the eyes to see the sacredness of nature that is often looked over.

Looking Back to Move Forward

Time is a spiral. In addition to our life lessons, time can spiral forward with our ancestors of our faith, our family, and those we love who have gone before us. While the notion of karma keeps some people thinking too much about past events and their repercussions, a spiraling forward as it relates to our ancestors means that we can continue on with the legacy they started. We, as guardians of the faith, can choose to continue on in the legacy of the mystics and prophets who have gone before us. We, as guardians of the faith, can choose to continue on in the legacy of Christ, taking our love out into communities.

We, as guardians of the faith, can carry the mantle of justice and reconciliation. We can choose to love our neighbor as we love ourselves, making sure that we honor our self-love and our self-care. We, as guardians of the faith, can call upon the saints who have gone before us who were harmed, killed, or forgotten. We, as guardians of the faith, can choose to treat women with honor, dignity, and respect. We don't need to repeat the cycle from those who were asleep to the oppressive patterns they continued. We can awaken, rise, and choose another way! We, as guardians of the faith, can choose at any time to reclaim our faith by making decisions that advance us forward from the lessons of the past. We have sovereignty. We have agency!

THE REBIRTH AND RISE OF THE UNIVERSAL MYSTIC

I have awakened the little girl in me that used to swing on the back porch and talk to the angels, fairies, and the spirits in nature. I would sing songs to them knowing they were listening. They are with me now. I hear them and they hear me.

I used to keep my spiritual wisdom to myself. Like a woman's crossed legs and folded arms, I knew to keep it small and contained on the outside. Because on the inside, my spiritual wisdom never fit in the tidy containers of just one denomination or religion. I'm done hiding the mystic ways of seeing God's ways. I want to share the fruits of the Spirit as I experience them, because they taste so sweet.

For millennia, cultures around the world have defined magic as that which is unseen. Unicorns, gnomes, dragons, and fairies all lie just beyond our realm of existence. Many of us have been drawn to the mystical and the magical, that which is beyond our physical vision.

But what I have come to realize is that the magical is unseen because it's within us. *We* are the magical ones.

Think of that flower that blooms. The flower has everything that it needs to bloom all in that little seed. From just a tiny seed, a stem rises above the ground and it becomes so much more than the little seed. Everything it needs to bloom is contained within the seed. It just needs a certain amount of energy from Source: water and light. In the same way, when we are connected to the Source of Love—to Spirit—then we too will bloom. We get to decide how big our bloom will be. I have experienced that we can decide when and how and what color, even. We can learn, and then decide, how to funnel our magic. We can help to shape the energy of Divine Love to become our bloom, our co-creation.

I hope the inspiring potential—the magic—that I feel in my heart is also being experienced by you. I pray that these words are imbued with a divine understanding so that we finally understand the significance that *we are the magical ones!* The spark of divinity is in *you*. Christ abides in you! We are able to shape our lives far beyond what we have been told. We are beloved, far beyond what we feel when events in our life allow shame and doubt to seep in. Guardians, step into the possibilities that arise when you know that Christ abides in you!

Perhaps there are mystical realms where gnomes and fairies really exist. I'm certainly open to the mystery of God and the wisdom revealed in other cultures. But what I am most in awe of and enthralled with is the notion that *we* are the magical ones. And we don't realize it! We don't see that the makings of our bloom (of what we wish to co-create) is also on the inside, like the flower. There is a universe within us when we acknowledge our divinity from within—the Christ that abides in us. I have learned to unlock it for me, and I hope you will take what you need from this book and embark on a journey to learn how to unlock your magic. Some of the keys for you might be different than what works for me, but what I am convinced of is that you have the wisdom within you to discover that magic.

Guardian of the faith, awaken the mystic in *you*. Allow yourself to believe that since Divine Love is in you, the magic is in you. Awaken to the possibility that we are only just beginning to understand humanity's potential, and the key is to liberate our concept of how interconnected we are with the power of God. It's time for the mystics to rise again. Will you rise with me?

The Sacred, Yet Common Meal

My mystic Christ eyes have allowed me to perceive Holy Communion differently; this understanding spirals around my original understanding. My understanding of the sacrament of Holy Communion is not less than it once was, but it has expanded. One could assume that how I was treated in the church spoiled the meaning of Holy Eucharist for me—but it did not. I still believe that the sacrament of Holy Communion is beautiful, sacred, and lovely. I believe it reveals the presence of Christ. What has changed over time is my understanding of the common meal. I now see and feel the sacredness of the common meal. Holy Communion doesn't mean anything less to me, but I now see that the mystic Christ is present every time we break bread and are aware of the presence of Christ in our midst. In Luke 22:19, Jesus took bread and at the Last Supper said, "This is my body, which is given for you. Do this in remembrance of me." Do you think he intended that to mean only on Sunday mornings, and only when ordained clergy say those words in church? I think he meant *let us remember him every time we eat and drink*. Every time. Church has institutionalized and taken ownership of those words, but I don't believe that was Jesus' exclusive intent. I have experienced many meals where I remember Christ outside of Holy Eucharist. That does not mean I value Holy Eucharist less.

Now I see beauty and sacredness in the world and in the breaking of bread around *any* table, including my table at home. My remembrance is an awareness. My remembrance is being conscious of Christ in all things, including the food I eat. Now the mystic in me wants to experience *more* of God's sanctuary in the world. I want to live out my days experiencing that same sacredness in a variety of ways in the world: through music, food, stories, experiences of awe and delight, gatherings of friends, and listening to other people's encounters with God specific to their culture and religion. It's all holy to me!

I will always be grateful for my upbringing and for the preciousness of the vast majority of my encounters in church, and for the privilege to administer holy sacraments.

Now, it is the sacredness of the ordinary that my eyes see anew.

The mystic Christ allows me to see the world as sanctuary and all of life as sacrament. It is okay for all of us, Christians too, to have changing, growing, and expanding concepts. Not linear, but evolving. Will you evolve with me, guardian of the faith? There is nowhere God is not!

The little girl that grew up playing in the forest finally got her magic back. Now, when I connect with Divine Love in others, I feel the magic in the world. I feel hope and renewal. I see God everywhere, in all of my life, in all of the people I love, and in the future potential that is before us now. God doesn't have to feel like a burden. God can feel like dawn after a dark night. God can feel like a newborn baby. God can feel like synchronicity, compassion, warmth, and magic. God can be found in the everydayness of life and the world. Awaken to the universal mystic and see the world through the eyes of a child who believes that anything is possible!

THE REBIRTH OF THE LOVER OF THE REJECTED

I experienced such joy in loving and serving those who were rejected when I was growing up. But as time spirals around, I became the rejected. Life has led me on a journey to love myself, even though I experienced rejection. And in many ways, the teachings of Jesus and the church have inspired me to more deeply love the rejected—the millions of people who have left the church, feeling rejected by shame and judgement. I think about them a lot.

As a child, I enjoyed serving up warm meat and veggies on those compartmentalized plates to those who were homeless. I can smell the food now. Today, I want to co-create a future church that can offer so much more to people that feel excluded, left out, and rejected. The banquet of God is magnificent, and it awaits you. You don't need to enter into a church to experience it, particularly if that was where you were rejected. But church has access to this banquet too. This banquet is everywhere. It is for you. God longs for you to taste it. You are invited to the feast; you are welcome to God's table. You are worthy, and you are good.

Time is a spiral, and now, loving and serving the rejected is no longer "them" and "me." I have experienced my own time as one of the ones that was rejected, and I learned to love myself, despite the judgements that others made about me. Once we come close to our own woundedness, it becomes impossible to see others as "them." We are all interconnected. There have been periods in my life where I needed to center my own care, my own self-compassion, and my own healing. And when that period ended, I was ready, once again, to spend time caring for those in the community who have been rejected as well. And for us as mamas and parents, we understand all too well the need to balance care for ourselves and care for our children, who are always needing our love, our care, our acceptance, and our compassion. At the end of it all, it's less a linear model of "us" serving "them." When we recognize our unity, then it becomes a more circular model of mutual belonging and community. I have been unequivocally blessed by relationships with people who are in need, food insecure, or housing insecure. In the height of my own rejection by good church folk who felt good about judging me, I felt community in the midst of others who were rejected by society.

Guardian of the faith, will you join me at the banquet of God? Will you step into mutuality as we serve and love those who have been rejected, including ourselves?

Claim Your Self-Worth

A patriarchal society (and many times, a patriarchal church) convinces women (and men) that they aren't enough. When we're told we are not enough, we often chase after validation. This can include validation in the form of how our bodies look; it can be in the form of makeup, clothes, accessories, and altering the shape of our face and bodies. We can chase after validation in the form of degrees, jobs, doing too much, or taking on an unbalanced approach in the family when responsibilities should be shared by others. Underneath all of that is the desire to be validated, because we have been raised in a society that tells us we're not enough as we are.

One of the most important things we can do as guardians of the faith is to claim our worth for ourselves. Don't wait for anyone else to tell you that you are enough. Even if they say you are enough, that will not be enough for you unless you come to a place on your own where you *believe* you are worthy as you are. Take the time that you need to settle in with the understanding that your very *being* is enough. You do not need to do more to earn your worth. You certainly don't need to do more than the men in your life. You don't need to achieve anything. You are enough as you are!

The love that you have is enough. That concept alone is a big shift for many of us. Not everyone that loves you will be ready to come alongside you in support of your spiritual expansion in that regard. When you share that you are on a journey toward seeking less validation, of taking some time for you even as you love to serve others, know that some people will react. Some people will reject; some people will flare up. But hold firm in that because your self-validation is a rock. After all, the way you love yourself is how you love others, so when we're exhausted and overworking, we're actually not loving others to the best of our ability. I can love others better and serve others better when I take time for myself and when I honor the Sabbath by taking a day to rest, renew my spirit by reconnecting with God, and being with loved ones.

Society especially loves to tell older women that they lack worth. I'm a middle-aged woman with a few wrinkles around my eyes and, like so many women, I've spent decades hearing messaging about losing weight, firming up wrinkles, and altering my appearance. Some would say I'm beyond the prime of my life because I'm no longer in the childbearing stage. But I know that in some ways, I'm just getting started. I've got the ancestors whose bones have been forgotten behind me. The women who have signed NDAs—even if they cannot speak, their energy is behind me.

Society might tell us one thing about ourselves, but God tells us another.

I'm just getting started. How about you? Can we be behind each other, letting God and ourselves determine our self-worth?

Loving All of Me, and Others

The lover of the rejected returned. And she returned when I learned to love myself fully, flaws and all. I learned to love the shadow side of me. I came to a place of loving the wounded woman in me who longed to be loved by her church but was instead rejected. I learned to love the woman I was in my past that stumbled while in a place of trauma when a man harmed me. I came to a place of total compassion and love for the woman I was years ago, who froze and was initially afraid to ask for help, afraid again to stand up. I came to a place of total love for the shadow part of me—for the woman in me who was so worried about reputation versus dignity. I had confused the two. I was overly concerned with my reputation, which is what others think of me, but I had dignity in the name of Christ the entire time. When I came to love (not judge) the shadow side of me and when I came to love (not judge) the rejected side of me, it allowed me to more deeply love those who are rejected in our society. Except this time, I could come close to them. I wanted to touch them and know their names, just like when I served lunch to people who were homeless when I was growing up. For now, I knew that I wasn't interested in "loving the rejected" in a hands-off way like through an outreach committee or by a financial donation, removed from personal interaction. The lover of the rejected returned, because first I learned to love the parts of me that had been rejected by others. I learned that God's love will never reject me for who I am or what happened to me. There are many of us who have been rejected by others for unjust reasons, including Jesus himself. I learned to never mistake people's judgements about me for the way I am seen through the eyes of God. We are all loved extravagantly, endlessly, and unconditionally. Every single one of us. God knows the very essence of who we are and loves us.

Arise, guardian! Arise into a greater love for the rejected, for you, for others, and for the world.

GUARDIAN, HONOR YOUR DIVINE RHEMA

Divine Rhema about Hierarchy

Claim your role as a guardian in relationship to hierarchy. Hierarchy is a part of nature and the animal kingdom. It is simply a reality. The purpose of hierarchy is to protect. But when decisions are made in the dark to protect the institution rather than the people who have been harmed, then the purpose of hierarchy has been abused. As guardians, we must pay attention to the culture of church-as-business. To be clear, there is nothing wrong with business. There are numerous ethical business owners, and businesses help make the world go round. Church-as-business refers to churches that put money ahead of the cause of Christ. The challenge with professionalizing Christianity is that we need to be mindful of the practical side of operations, income, and assets, and yet, that can never be a priority over following Christ without harm to others. That is the challenge and we get it wrong too often. As guardians, we must guard against this happening. We do that by expecting transparency at every turn.

In a healthy church hierarchy, the people at the top should be guardians to make sure that business (if you call it that) is done in accordance with the teachings of Christ, who centered the poor, the wounded, and the excluded. In Christian hierarchy, those at the top have the responsibility of honoring the upside-down world shown to us by Jesus. This means that Christian leaders in hierarchical positions need to wrestle with what it looks like to be at the top of an organization seeking to follow Jesus, when Jesus brought himself down low.

Ironically, Jesus himself paved the way for the role of the guardian to belong not only at the top but all up and down the hierarchy. Jesus was always inviting the humble and the rejected into positions of power and voice. He invited disciples who were lowly fishermen into the role of guardians of the faith. Shepherds who heard of Jesus' birth were entrusted as guardians to tell others. It was Jesus who went beyond the typical roles of hierarchy and empire so that everyday folk were considered the guardians of his teachings. He changed the game by empowering people like you and me who didn't have a lot of societal power. He gave them authority in the name of Christ and entrusted them to share the faith they had and become guardians of the faith.

We (those of us who are people of faith but without hierarchical power or societal power) need to take our power back as guardians, speaking up when injustice takes place and speaking out when our faith has been abused.

For too long we have given our power away to a church that has been all too comfortable holding on to that power.

To be clear, I am not advocating doing away with hierarchy. In fact, I believe Jesus can move through hierarchical systems because I believe the power of God can move through any people, anywhere people desire to honor God. And yet we do need to wake up, speak up, and carefully discern which hierarchical organizations we want to be a part of based on where their people power goes, where their money goes, how are they directly impacting people in the world in a spirit of Christ's love, how are they facing their shadow sides, and how thoroughly they honor the faith they espouse—both in public and in private. It's time we ask the hard questions! It's time we seek transparency. Demand the information. Step into our power as guardians of the faith! The church is nothing without members, congregants, parishioners, and those who show up and give.

I didn't feel safe "inside the church" after what happened to me. I tried for some time to come to a place of feeling safe and secure. The vast majority of people inside the church are not the problem. The problem is the values of the hierarchical system operating behind the scenes that seeks to hide and protect their shadow side. So let us be gentle with (most) people, and firmer with church-as-business. We, who are entrusted to being guardians of the faith (which is all of us), need to decide where our loyalty lies. Are we loyal to an institution even if it puts itself above the values of Christ? Or are we loyal to being a guardian of the faith passed down to us by our ancestors and by Christ? Perhaps you will become a guardian of the faith who stays within our hierarchies, insisting on reform from the inside. Or perhaps you will be a guardian that follows Jesus far beyond church walls. You get to decide.

Divine Rhema: Moving beyond Baby Christianity

In order to get beyond baby Christianity,[42] we must go beyond being spoon-fed by our mother, father, or our pastor. At some point we progress beyond baby food and we graduate from toddling to walking, to running, to racing and climbing, to playing and soaring. In the next stage, we choose the food that we will put in our mouth. We decide what spiritual teachings are nourishing for us and rooted in love. We decide what we like and we become much more independent. We learn how to say yes and no, and we don't feel guilty about not taking in the beliefs that don't sit right with us. A loving parent encourages freedom to explore our boundaries, knowing that we are safe. Our Divine Father and Divine Mother want to see us spiritually advance. It's okay to not want to be spoon fed anymore.

Listening to the divine rhema from God allows us to go directly to the Source of all of Creation—straight to God, straight to Jesus. I can call on the powers that be to give me clarity, teachings, comfort, strength, and signs and synchronicities. I am being shown how to be a guardian for a faith that is much more expansive than any institution can grasp. You too can go straight to God, straight to Jesus, straight to your angels. Claim your worth as a guardian. Be faithful to the Word, to listening to God, and you too will be shown how to become a guardian.

Divine Rhema: Take Back Your Power

As I look patriarchy in the eyes, let me tell you this: In the eyes of God, we are the same. We are not loved more by God if we have more titles, more theology degrees, or more authority in the church. Release the man-made layers in between you and God. No matter if we are ordained or not, no matter our education level, no matter whether we wear church robes or whether we are standing in the front of the church leading, or sitting in pews or chairs, or walking in the woods, or holding someone we love: we each are equally capable of listening to God in our hearts. We are equally capable of listening to the Christ that abides within. For too long we have given our authority away. I'm not only looking at patriarchy, but I'm looking into *your* eyes, dear reader, to say this:

Take back your power!

Take back your authority!

Liberate yourself from the shackles of institutional religion if they are limiting your concept of God. Because Jesus and God are certainly present all around us, and there is nothing that we need outside of ourselves and one another, to draw near to God. The concept of "church" should no longer be limited to church buildings with staff, denominations, corporate religious institutions, and non-profits. "Church" can simply be defined as where two or three or more are gathered together. And you are entitled to simply draw near to God in the silence of your heart any time you want. As you do this with regularity, you will begin to trust the way that God is speaking to your heart. Simply ask God to speak to you in a way that you will understand. Ask God to speak a word that is clear. And you will know that it is of God when that word feels pure and full of love for you.

THE REBIRTH OF THE SPIRITUAL WARRIOR

The Spiritual Warrior came back. Except this time, I have laid down her gloves. I have been through chrysalis, a transformation. I no longer carry the energy of a fighter nor that of a victim. I AM stepping into my power as a guardian. I AM a guardian of the faith. I stand exactly where I AM with the confidence of a fierce girl ready to fight the boys in a karate tournament. But now I AM guarding and protecting the faith of my ancestors. Guarding the beautiful faith of my great-grandfather, Justo; my great-grandmother, Mercy; my grandmothers, Belia and Betty; my grandfathers, Raoul and Bob. They did not pass down the faith of Jesus Christ through family and to me so that it could be spoiled by misogyny, lies, corruption, control, and deceit. I am a guardian of the faith in my heart, a guardian of the faith of my family, and a guardian who summons the energies of renewal, revolution, and reform.

As a guardian of the faith, I pray this prayer, looking squarely at the patriarchy of generations that have harmed and are harming others, in the name of Christ. I invite you to join me:

Sacred Creator of the Universe,

The spark of Christ that abides in me calls out to you. My cries pierce through the folds of the universe. I call upon the ancestors of our faith to join me. I call upon the spirits of the women executed as witches, the women tried as adulterers when they were harmed. I call upon the spirits of Justo's bones. I call upon the spirits of slaves, now free in the realm of heaven. I call upon the spirits of generations of people who have experienced harm in the name of Jesus. I call upon the angels of God. I call upon the great religious leaders of faiths around the world. I call upon the power of Jesus Christ. With all the love in my heart, I cry out: join together and help us!

Awaken in us the ability to right the wrongs of our faith. Join your collective power together with our desire to create another way that is truer to Christ's will. Move in us to reform our faith. Empower us to demand a faith of integrity and justice, dignity, compassion, and love.

Move in us to create a faith that is for all of us, including women. Help us to create a faith where women are more than second-class citizens, where our gifts are valued, where our emotions are revered, and where our intelligence, our bodies, and our spirits are respected and honored. Show us how to honor and integrate the Divine Feminine qualities that have been repressed. Show us what Divine Masculine qualities can look like in a more noble form. Show us how to raise and advance our faith to a higher way than what we have now.

Empower us to be guardians and protectors of our faith and our spirituality to ensure that joy and love are front and center. Empower us to ensure that the energy of harmony and peace resides in our hearts, in our relationships, and in our communities.

I know this will take a miracle. But I believe in miracles. I've seen you work a miracle in me and others, Great Spirit. I've seen the way your Christ light shines through the cracks of our once-shattered hearts. I've seen the way you raise up the broken. May your Christ light also shine through the cracks of our broken faith. May leaders fall to their knees in humility, with the desire for reform. May the voice of those who have been injured and are silent, cry out in a choir whose collective voices echo across the nations, ushering in a new creation in Christ. May followers of Jesus follow him out into their communities, following him, not for the sake of membership or tithes, but to spread Christ's love in our aching world.

We need renewal, not a stewardship campaign. We need revolution, not another church program. We need justice, not nuanced statements to protect an institution. I appeal to you now because church as business chooses business above the heart of Christ.

I pray to you, also, for a new season of our faith to emerge, one in which we are all guardians of Love, rather than warriors for one way. I pray for a new season of respect for faiths around the world. Help us to honor the sacred wisdom of God in many cultures, listening and learning from one another. Laying down weapons and joining hands. For when we unite in our desire to honor you, Sacred Creator, we can change the world with your guidance.

If anything is possible, make this possible. Move in us and through us, we who sincerely yearn for another way. Guide every step. Work a miracle in us, the broken open. We know "this extraordinary power belongs to God and does not belong to us."[43] *And yet we pray that the extraordinary power in each of our hearts that belongs to you, God, may be combined, echoing through the universe as Jesus prayed for the past, the present, and the future. We pray this boldest of prayers with a spirit of humility, knowing that it will only be through your great power and your amazing grace that a new way is resurrected among us.*

Amen.

Pausing to Reflect

As a guardian of our faith, I pause to reflect. I reflect with deep gratitude on the many ways that church has held me, formed me, and shaped me. I reflect with deep gratitude on my childhood, my family whom I love so dearly, and our stories. I reflect with gratitude on the thousands of individuals in the church I know that inspire me and have formed me. I reflect on the many, many people I know who have left the church out of care for themselves. I pause, allowing myself to reflect on the times I was hurt. Hurt by men, hurt by a lack of transparency, hurt by clergy and parishioners, and hurt to realize that church-as-business is part of the reality of things at this moment in our history. I lament. I lament not only our history and the present ways we fall short, but I lament the ways I have unknowingly participated in this system. I also forgive, but not without calling for and working for reform and a new way. I forgive the church, I forgive people in the church pews, and I forgive church leaders. I forgive myself, too. I give thanks to Christ, who always helps me to forgive more deeply when a pang in my heart shows me it's time for another level of forgiveness.

I see it all now, with Christ's eyes. I see my own healing journey and spiritual expansion toward loving myself and others, and loving the church. I hold a deeper compassion and I'm hopeful for what is to come. My Christ eyes have allowed me to see the presence of God in new ways. I feel God's presence everywhere now. I can be aware of God's presence through Christ consciousness. I can listen deeply for wisdom from the Christ that abides in me when I listen for divine rhema. And by seeking beyond a one-dimensional understanding of God, I have begun to experience a side of God that patriarchal Christianity does not emphasize, which for me is the Divine Mother. My love of Christ has deepened. My love of God continues—only now I have given myself permission to acknowledge that church as we know it has a shadow side that oppresses others, and to imagine, pray, and work for a wider concept of church that strives for more transparency, reform, a deeper impact in our communities, and to empower people of faith to directly communicate and listen to God who is much more expansive than we have perceived.

I embrace the expansiveness of life and of my spiritual journey. I no longer desire to fit into anyone's box, nor do I desire to judge anyone who is nourished by their church. Our great God can move through hierarchy or no hierarchy, church pews or concerts, inside church walls or beyond church walls, in the forest or by a lake. In a cathedral or in a backyard. There is truly nowhere God is not. Since I know this to be true, I embrace the desire to continually expand my understanding of God. Let me spend the rest of my life experiencing how God moves in the lives of other cultures, other faiths, other music, other wisdom, and other people! Let me spend the rest of my days seeking to deepen my compassionate love for others in a variety of ways that take me far beyond church walls. Let my mind, my heart, and my feet keep on exploring and expanding to discover new realms since God is in the midst of it all! How do Carl Jung's interpretations of synchronicity compare to mine? What does Paramahansa Yogananda say about the second coming of Christ and how does that parallel with my own divine rhema?

Why did early Christianity shut out a belief in reincarnation and what about the millions of us who sense that a belief in Jesus and in reincarnation can coexist just fine? It's time to step into the power of *my* experiences. Like the time I was on a beach in Mexico with my husband and we were receiving massages side by side in a quaint hut, with the sound of the ocean in the background. I was on my stomach, relaxing with my eyes closed when the woman massaging me gently bent my right arm behind my back. Immediately I tensed up and the still small voice clearly said, "Relax—you are safe. You were persecuted and your life ended once with your hands tied behind you like this. But this is a new energy and *this* time, your hands are behind you as you receive a gentle massage on the beach. Things are different now." It's time to own *my* truth, even (and perhaps especially) if it doesn't fit into the traditional box of Christianity. There have been times in my life when my divine rhema has shown me insights into past lives and past parts of this life and how I spiral forward in spiritual advancement. I will continue to embrace and trust my journey and my insights, knowing that it's all held by God.

I want to explore gnostic books and read the scripture that was left out of the Bible. I will lean into my own discernment and critical thinking and explore what I think about the words and life of Jesus. I want to explore what patriarchal Christianity has left out and ask *why*. What does the whole story look like? I want to learn about people's near-death experiences and listen to my friends' experiences of their kundalini awakenings. This exploration feels good and right to me, not because what I know isn't enough, but because there are so many other perspectives, stories, and cultures that provide a richer and fuller understanding of God. How can I cultivate my ability to heal myself and the world? I want to always keep exploring—traveling to countries and praying in ashrams, temples, churches, and mosques, dancing and singing in other languages, and feasting with people of faith around the world! Poring over books and being expanded through conversation with people who aren't like me at all. I don't want to confine myself in any way because God doesn't confine God's self to one religion or one place in time. God is always appearing! Wandering can be a sign of faithfulness—it is certainly that for me.

Since I know there is nowhere God is not, I stand in solidarity with the many, many people who prefer to stay on the margins of church or outside the church. I stand in solidarity with the many who are on the margins of society. On the margins of being included. On the margins of whatever they long for. For God is with us too. We, too, are church.

I give thanks for the past, even as I walk with a new energy into a future that is unknown. I let go of the energies of guilt, shame, and striving to fit in. I feel ease and flow when I stay in alignment with the living Christ in my life. My very being unfolds as a flower that is equally soft and strong. Love flows. Love is soft and strong. I have released the energy of the aggressive warrior and the traumatized victim. Perhaps you are ready to step into a new energy, too. Living into Christ consciousness means that we are experiencing the current energy of the eternal Now, which is not struggle and hardship. We are on the brink of what is emerging.

Labor Pains: The Great Birth That Is Occurring

I have seen and experienced what is happening on a collective level for so many people who seek to experience God outside of structure, institutions, and church buildings. I have heard from countless individuals and groups that are experiencing a spiritual awakening, or a heightened perception of Spirit moving in the world and in their lives. It's as though many of us are now open to seeing the world with new eyes—with the eyes of Christ consciousness. I feel joy at the thought that my spiritual awakening is not alone—that there are others! And I wonder: what could society look like when large populations of people seek to deeply listen to God who abides within? What could it look like when our spirits are uniting together to listen to one another's wisdom and rhema in order to solve the world's problems of suffering, inequity, and injustice? What does it look like when our lives slow down and we value relationships over consumption and overwork? What are the shifts that are underway in us as individuals and how can we do this together, in community? Oh the *joy* we will experience when we truly see one another as the Christ-that-abides-in-you, the Christ-that-abides-in-me, and the Christ-that-abides-in-us.[44]

Rise Up, Guardians, and Embrace This Time!

In proclaiming the great birth that is about to occur, I can feel the labor pains. I have sensed this growing in the womb of creation and it's time for this birth. We feel the constriction. We feel the labor pains. Upheaval and change is in the air. It seems like old constructs are breaking open while we are in the painful process of birthing new ways of being. It started small, but this rising up has been growing and now it's running out of room. It's starting to feel uncomfortable. We are in the last trimester, tired, weary, and restless. And oh, how labor hurts! We scream with agony, tears rolling down our cheeks. Give us an epidural to numb the fear and pain of our hearts!

Labor pains are never easy. As we enter into a period of pain and breaking open, we seek to have faith like Mary, knowing that what is coming will be so beautiful. So let us proclaim with goodness the reign of Christ consciousness! We sing with joy for the deep awareness of the Christ that abides in you and me and the ways that it will shift and change the world! Justice rolls down when we see our fellow neighbor, man, woman, and child as one of us. There will be enough manna for *all* when our deep compassion rises up, blanketing our scarcity with hope and abundance.

When we speak from the wisdom from within, our voices will proclaim new solutions to problems we thought couldn't be solved, new models of leadership will emerge, and new ways of thinking and perceiving the world will be welcomed and embraced.

This will disrupt the status quo. Labor pains, too, disrupt. So I write in hopes that my pen will break the waters and promote the birth of this next era, to usher in the *Great Renewal* for all of us, not only the church. We feel constriction and our hearts are beating louder. We are not looking forward to the labor but we do look forward to the other side of it. We are ready to step into it. In fact, some of us are already dancing and singing with joy!

We are singing like the birds in the midst of a lush forest. We are dancing like insects on shimmering water. We are skipping and leaping like children around a fire, full of joy and without care or concern for what others think! We are dancing because there's plenty to eat and drink for all. We are dancing because our souls are equally honored. We are dancing because the mystic Christ has returned in each of us. We are singing because our faith is led by love, compassion, justice, equality, and a reverence for the earth, the animals, the land, for people, and finally—*finally*, for women. I am singing. We are singing! We're singing because we see life now, in a new way. Will you join us in your own tune, in your own way? Let our voices sing in harmony and rise, together.

Guardians, Spread Your Wings!

When the lens through which we were taught to view the world begins to crack, and then shatters and breaks open, it is impossible at first to see through our own devastation. But gradually a new way of seeing and understanding, more beautiful than before, will emerge like the dawn after a long, dark night.

As a child I was told I wouldn't be able to walk by the time I was forty. Not only can I walk, I have learned how to fly. As an adult, struggling with trauma and pain from the harm I endured in the church, I was told I would always be weakened, limited, and burdened by what happened to me. But I have experienced the miracle of healing. I know of death and now, resurrection. And for centuries—for thousands of years—we've been told that life was a certain way. We were raised within constructs that benefit a few, while keeping so many of us small and limited in our potential. We have been kept from knowing our divinity from within, like being in a locked room with thick curtains covering the light and the view outside the walls. But those constructs have cracks in them now. We are pulling back the curtains and taking them down. We are venturing beyond walls, and a more beautiful paradigm is emerging and coming into view. The key was within us all along.

I've been experimenting with using my wings—the ones that no one told me I had because they didn't know they had them either. I've been on a spiritual journey, flying amongst the shadows of night, while others are asleep. And here I am, still catching my breath from my journey amongst the stars and sky, excited to share good news for anyone with eyes to see and ears to hear: I have seen the dawn rising from distant lands! I have seen Her expansive, radiant aura rising from the wide horizon: a gold glow that lights up the entire sky bringing us hope that the new way we have longed for is finally here. I soared all the way here, accompanied by hawk and eagle, being carried by wind, eager to tell you, for we have been in the dark for so long:

The dawn is coming! I've seen Her light and felt Her warmth myself. With Her light I could see my wings for the first time. With Her guidance I have learned how to soar. Christ consciousness guided me to Her, giving me eyes to see undiscovered realms where the Word has always been. Let us not stand still, waiting for Her to come to us. Come fly with me. Come see these new realms illumined by Her radiance. Come see another face of our one God. You have wings too, you know. Let us soar together, toward Her, carried by wind, by Spirit, by Divine Love. Unimaginable beauty awaits us all.

Reflection Questions: Chapter 10

- What does it feel like to imagine and consider yourself as a guardian of our faith? What images come to mind when you think of a guardian. What are you guarding or protecting? What kind of qualities does a guardian have?
- What is it like to imagine understanding the earth as sanctuary and all of life as sacramental (an outward, visible sign of an inward, spiritual grace)?
- As guardians of the faith, what are some ways we can step into mutuality as we serve and love those who have experienced rejection, including ourselves?
- What steps can you take on the journey toward seeking less validation? Can you make the connection between your ability to love others better and taking care of your own needs, without concern for what others think?
- What is a hard question you would like to ask of a church you are familiar with that is patriarchal, hierarchical, and/or traditional in its leadership? What is preventing you from asking that question?
- What would you add to the prayer to the Sacred Creator of the Universe? Can you join me in praying this prayer?
- What do you sense are the spiritual shifts that are underway in us as individuals? How can we do this together, in community?

11

Meeting the Cosmic Mother Within

I AM

I AM Mother Nature
I AM her and She is me
Her air resides in my lungs
Her water can be found in my tears, in my blood, in my veins
Her fire can be found in my soul, in the heat of me
Her earth is my skin, my hair, my nails.
I AM Mother Nature and She is me
We are One
Goddess, Divine Mother, Queen in Her
Goddess, Divine Mother, Queen in me
The waters of my womb that washed over their births
Became my children's baptism into Love
My milk was their first Communion, the essence of Life
Perfect sustenance that nurtures miracles
My eyes, the candles that drew them closer to the divine
My love was the Divine Love that gave them life
My body was their home

Their temple, their sanctuary
My arms are the arms of the Goddess
I embrace Her with my love
I embrace ALL children with my love
With these arms
My intellect is the cosmos
I am Nature and She is me
She nurtures Life, as do I
She sustains Life, as do I
My heartbeat, my rhythms, and movements
Move with the ebbs and flow of nature.
My flow yields to the cycle of the moon
To the tides of the ocean
My mind rises with the sun
My intuition rises with the moon
My curves are foothills and mountains.
A soft place to rest
Symbols of abundance and goodness
I rest like the winter, bare and still
I bloom like the summer, warm and fragrant
I nurture, I birth, I yield, I renew, like the earth
Like the Cosmic Mother.

COSMIC MOTHER

I am the cosmic mother of all
My eyes are constellations of the soul
My blood is the river of life
My womb births life and death. The cycle of life resides in *me*
I AM a creator of life
I am the cosmic mother of all

All children can find a home with me
My arms extend to you
My nurturing love is safe
My compassion is as deep as the ocean

Come to me, you children who have forgotten your mother
I have been waiting for your return
Awaken to the Goddess's love
Let me heal your heart
Let me bring ease to your rough journey
Let me bind the wounds of your brokenness

You will see I AM everywhere when you awaken to me
My song can be heard when the bird sings
My movement is as gentle as a cool stream of water
Rest in my shade beneath the trees.
Release your sorrows in the fire
Pray as you walk
I hear your quietest longings, your emotion, your sorrow, your heartache
I hear your hope, your gladness
It is all welcome. It is all a part of life. Bring it to me for nothing—
Nothing can separate me from you

You will always be a part of me. I will always love you
Awaken to your Divine Mother's gentle, strong love
Awaken to the love, the home, and the heart of the Goddess
Awaken to her compassion that holds all of life in our natural world

She is everywhere. She is earth, in you, in me. There is nowhere She is not
Arise, Goddess within us, arise!

Awaken and look around
Sit quietly but awake. Conscious
Notice her. She is everywhere. Look in the mirror, deep in your eyes
Arise Goddess within us, arise!

EAGLE

Our lives are meant to soar with freedom
And ease
And Joy
My wings will not be clipped
I will not be caged
I will not be silenced
I will not be quiet
I will not be repressed
I will rise again
Redemption is my song!

A NEW ERA

Every sunrise announces my coming
This is a new era
The Goddess's love is open to each of us who are ready
For a new way of being
A way of compassion
A way of freedom
A way of ease
The resistance of oppression
Union with nature

The clarity of a lake, glimmering in the morning sun
A new day is dawning
She rises again
Let her speak to you
Let her come to you
Her arms are open
You can find them in your nearest forest
You can find them in a warm bath
You can find them around a fire at night
You can find them by watching the birds on a still morning
You can find her while fully immersed in the sea
You can find her in the sound of a river
You can find her in the dance of a butterfly
You can find her when you envelop a baby
You can find her when you hold an animal
You can find her when you lose yourself in love
You can find her in the moments that you often recall
"This is what life is about."
In those sacred moments
The promise that awaits you is this:
All of life is sacred
All of life can be full of these sacred moments
Go to her
Renew your connection with her
Awaken to the Goddess within you and all around you
Awaken to the Cosmic Mother
She is safe
She is home
There is nowhere She is not.

WE RISE AGAIN

I will not be silenced
She will not be silenced
I will not be repressed
She will not be repressed
I have been redeemed
She is redeeming
I have been healed
She is a great healer
I rise again
She rises again.

Reflection Questions:
Chapter 11

- What could help you to meet the Cosmic Mother within?
- What aspects of you parallel with nature, animals, the Divine Mother, or the Divine Father

EPILOGUE:

Return to the River

I have returned to the forest. How sweet it is to be loved by God and nurtured by Mother Earth. How sweet it is to come and receive her wisdom. I walk slowly, taking in the smell of life, the humming of insects in synchronicity with one another. I notice how the water reflects a shimmering light. Black dragonflies and monarch butterflies float and flutter across my path. I begin by approaching a humble bridge and sitting down. I notice and give thanks for all that surrounds me. I recall all the insights and wisdom I have received from the river and from animals, and the way they come to me in perfect timing. Like a sacramental rite (and it is, in every way, sacramental: an outward, visible sign of an inward, spiritual grace). I slowly rise and walk toward a path that has been blocked off by a chain. I go around the chain. If I am honest with myself, I have often chosen the path less traveled, and it calls to me once again. No footsteps have gone this way, so I follow the steps of the deer, whose hooves are clearly defined on the trail.

I gather two heavy stones, symbolic of specific things I'm ready to release to the water flowing away from me. They are jagged and heavy like the burdens I am releasing. I gather three yellow leaves that pop out to me in the midst of a sea of bright green in the woods during summer.

The leaves symbolize the lightness of my being, floating effortlessly in perfect flow with the river. I return to the wooden bridge.

As I stand on the bridge, I begin by turning toward the water flowing away from me. I begin thinking of what I am ready to let go of in my life. I begin: "I am already releasing others' expectations of me. Thank you for the protection that fitting in once provided. I no longer need it now. I am fully protected by God, by Christ light, by angels and spirit guides, by all that is Love. Thank you. I release you now." I throw the heavy rock in the river. The burden releases.

I take the second rock. "I am already releasing anything that stings. I am releasing lingering hurts and disappointments, both from others and myself. I release blockages. I am ready to flow like the river, fully connected with the current of God—the Source of All that is Love." I throw the rock far. It lands exactly where it needs to. Ripples on either side move the water. A heron takes flight. And the River of Life absorbs the ripples, encompassing it with love.

I turn the other way, toward the current of the river that is coming to me. Standing over the rail of the bridge, I drop my leaves in. One or two are beginning to brown at the edges, symbolic of my own peace with aging. As I let the leaves go, I notice how lightly they float, guided by a flow much greater than they are. They float without resistance. I welcome the perfect current that is the flow of the River of Life. I give thanks for all that the river has taught me. She has taught me about God's timing, as some parts of the river move fast, while other areas linger with movement, or are even stagnant. But everything eventually goes back to Source. She has taught me about abundance. She has taught me how to float and relax and trust the current. The pace of my life, too, is in accordance with God's will because I am willfully connected and in alignment with God's will in my life. The river is my teacher and I give thanks for her.

And one day, I know, I too will return to the great River of Life. Once again, I will return to the Source of All Creation. One day I will shed this body like a snake sheds old skin, and my soul will merge with the Love that encompasses the universe. I'll be thankful for all these times I experienced God through others, through nature, and through me. I will guide my children and grandchildren and loved ones on Earth from this higher perspective now. They will know I'm with them when feathers cross their path unexpectedly, when the hawk soars over them just as they have an insight or idea they should pursue. They will know I'm with them when a little ladybug gently makes her appearance in their home. When it is time to rejoin my one, brilliant light with the great Light that is Love, I will merge with other bright lights. I will recognize my ancestors, the ones who came before me. We will be in holy communion, a kirtan, in ecstatic dance, moving to the flow of Love in us and all around us. I will be home. And yet, I am home here, and now, in this very moment. Because there is nowhere God is not.

AFTERWORD:

An Invitation for the Spiral Fractal to Continue through You

Dear Reader,

This book is ending, and yet a new beginning awaits. Would you like a partner as you practice the teachings in *Following Jesus Beyond Church Walls*? I want to personally encourage you to invite others to join a circle with you to learn from one another and share stories and experiences. The purpose of these groups is to cultivate community and nurture friendships in a supportive environment as individuals practice the teachings found in this book.

Visit chantalmckinney.com, where you can receive resources for starting a circle in your community, and sign up to join online community and conversations related to *Following Jesus Beyond Church Walls*.

More than nurturing friendships, we "love our neighbor as our self." My hope is that these supportive in-person and online communities lead to a deeper love of God, which includes the ability to more deeply love and care for the self and the desire to love and serve our communities. Through my website, circles will receive resources to be a tangible blessing to the community in which they live, and can be connected to other circles, creating a networked, grassroots community of people increasing God's reign of Love.

It is my sincere desire that these communal offerings are an ongoing blessing to individuals and the community around you. My prayer and deepest intention is that each reader experience the rich blessings found in both giving and receiving love from God, self, and neighbors. May our compassionate action transform the world around us, improving the livelihood of people everywhere and the wellbeing of our precious Earth. May the Source of All Love bless and be glorified by this humble endeavor to grow the reign of Love in our world, one person, one group, and one community at a time. I hope you will join us. chantalmckinney.com

With every blessing as you become a catalyst,

Chantal

APPENDIX:

Quotes from Religions and Faiths of the World[45]

Every blade of grass, every leaf and flower, every person, and every faith rooted in love allows us to know God. Every life experience can allow us to draw closer to the love of God in one another and in all of nature. There is nowhere God is not. There is nowhere Christ is not. It is, therefore, a worthy pursuit to expand our concept of God beyond one concept, one experience, and one faith. For our one God is the God of us all.
—CHANTAL MCKINNEY

In the beginning was the Word, and the Word was with God, and the Word was God. He was in the beginning with God. All things came into being through him, and without him not one thing came into being. What has come into being in him was life, and the life was the light of all

*people. The light shines in the darkness, and
the darkness did not overcome it.*
—JOHN 1:1–5

*When the earth is ravaged and the animals are dying,
a new tribe of people shall come unto the earth from
many colors, classes, creeds and who by their actions
and deeds shall make the earth green again. They
will be known as the warriors of the rainbow.*
—HOPI PROPHECY

God became man so that man might become God.
—ST. ATHANASIUS

*The eye with which I see God is the same
one with which God sees me.*
—MEISTER ECKHART

Abide in me as I abide in you.
—JESUS IN THE GOSPEL OF JOHN 15:4

*But we have this treasure in clay jars, so that it may be
made clear that this extraordinary power belongs to God
and does not come from us. We are afflicted in every way,
but not crushed; perplexed, but not driven to despair;
persecuted, but not forsaken; struck down, but not destroyed.*
—2 CORINTHIANS 2:7–9

*Among the few who possess inner strength to resist the
mass unconsciousness will rise a new neo-indigenous
people. Prophecies foretell of a people who will rise
from earth's ashes like the Thunderbird, symbolizing*

rebirth. They will bring balance and harmony back to Mother Earth. The first of these beings will come as teachers and storytellers to remind us of ancient truths of the star people and beyond. They will be pathfinders leading the way to a new universe, a new reality.

Great leaders, Warriors and Shamans of many nations will be born and they will cleanse the earth for rebirth. Next will come the Planters sowing seeds of truth, justice and freedom. The Storytellers, Warriors and Planters will live in the way of the Great Spirit and teach ways to keep Mother of the Ground sacred forevermore. They will be called Rainbow Warriors for they will gather the four sacred directions, all distinctly separate but forever connected in the Circle of Life."
—LEE STANDING BEAR MOORE, MANATAKA AMERICAN INDIAN COUNCIL

I ask not only on behalf of these, but also on behalf of those who will believe in me through their word, that they may all be one. As you, Father, are in me and I am in you, may they also be in us, so that the world may believe that you have sent me. The glory that you have given me I have given them, so that they may be one, as we are one, I in them and you in me, that they may become completely one, so that the world may know that you have sent me and have loved them even as you have loved me.
—JESUS PRAYING IN THE GOSPEL OF JOHN 17: 20–23

If you want to find the secrets of the universe, think in terms of energy, frequency, and vibration.
—NIKOLA TESLA

> *What we need most*
> *in order to make progress*
> *is to be silent*
> *before this great God*
> *with our appetite*
> *and with our tongue,*
> *for the language*
> *he best hears*
> *is silent love.*
> —JOHN OF THE CROSS, SAYINGS OF LIGHT
> AND LOVE, TRANS. MIRABAI STARR

> There is truth in the prophecies of the Rainbow and the Rainbow people. People from all of the Americas will unite with people from all the other nations, and they will realize that we are all Family, brothers and sisters. This is not my personal vision, but the cosmic vision presented by all the elders, a vision that we all share.
> —DON ALEJANDRO CIRILO PEREZ, MAYA ELDERS COUNCIL, GUATEMALA

MARY'S REBUKE TO THE CHURCH

I am like the rainbow above the clouds, which seem to stoop down and touch the earth with both ends, for I stoop down to the dwellers on earth and touch both bad and good by my prayers—the good, that they may be faithful to the bidding of Holy Church, their Mother; the bad that they may not continue to grow worse in their sins. I now make known to those to whom my words are sent that from one part of the earth terrible clouds are rising up against the brightness of the rainbow. Most of the ministers of the

Quotes from Religions and Faiths of the World

Church are sunk in worldly pleasure, the love of money, pomp, and pride. Their sins rise up from the earth to heaven against my prayers as the dark clouds come over the sky's bright rainbow...Such men out to be put down instead of being exalted in the Church. But whosoever will do his part in strengthening its foundations...and to renovate the holy vineyard that God has planted and watered... shall receive help from me, the Queen of heaven, and all the angelic host...The vineyard I speak of is God's Holy Church, which needs renewing in humility and divine charity.
—SAINT BRIDGET OF SWEDEN (1302–1373)

Write the vision; make it plain on tablets, so that a runner may read it. For there is still a vision for the appointed time; it speaks of the end, and does not lie. If it seems to tarry, wait for it; it will surely come, it will not delay. Look at the proud! Their spirit is not right in them, but the righteous live by their faith.
—HABAKKUK 2:2–4

Nothing in this world is as close to God as stillness.
—MEISTER ECKHART

In all your ways acknowledge God and God will direct your paths.
—PROVERBS 36

See, I make all things new.
—REVELATION 21:5

The Great Spirit is in all things. He is in the air we breathe. The Great Spirit is our Father, but the

> *Earth is our Mother. She nourishes us...That which we put into the ground she returns to us."*
> —BIG THUNDER WABANAKI, ALGONQUIN

> *Mother Earth is a goddess, venerated by indigenous peoples. Mother Earth is much more than the soil we walk on. It is the wind, the fire, the water, the element that we breathe and that sustains life and prosperity.*
>
> *Unfortunately, we're not doing much to protect her. The Pachamama, the Incan fertility goddess who presides over planting and harvesting, and embodies the mountains and causes earthquakes, is suffering.*
> —SISTER EDIA LÓPEZ, SISTERS OF MERCY,
> "MOTHER EARTH IS SACRED: WE ARE ONE"

> *"Every Christian is to become a little Christ. The whole purpose of becoming a Christian is simply nothing else."*
> —C.S. LEWIS, MERE CHRISTIANITY

THE GIFTS OF WISDOM

> *Does not wisdom call,*
> *and does not understanding raise her voice?*
>
> *On the heights, beside the way,*
> *at the crossroads she takes her stand;*
>
> *beside the gates in front of the town,*
> *at the entrance of the portals she cries out:*

Quotes from Religions and Faiths of the World

'To you, O people, I call,
and my cry is to all that live.

O simple ones, learn prudence;
acquire intelligence, you who lack it.

Hear, for I will speak noble things,
and from my lips will come what is right;

ᶠor my mouth will utter truth;
wickedness is an abomination to my lips.

All the words of my mouth are righteous;
there is nothing twisted or crooked in them.

They are all straight to one who understands
and right to those who find knowledge.

Take my instruction instead of silver,
and knowledge rather than choice gold;

for wisdom is better than jewels,
and all that you may desire cannot compare with her.
—PROVERBS 8:1–11

WISDOM'S PART IN CREATION

The Lord created me at the beginning[a] of his work,[b]
the first of his acts of long ago.

Ages ago I was set up,

at the first, before the beginning of the earth.
When there were no depths I was brought forth,
when there were no springs abounding with water.

Before the mountains had been shaped,
before the hills, I was brought forth—

when he had not yet made earth and fields,[c]
or the world's first bits of soil.

When he established the heavens, I was there,
when he drew a circle on the face of the deep,

when he made firm the skies above,
when he established the fountains of the deep,

when he assigned to the sea its limit,
so that the waters might not transgress his command,
when he marked out the foundations of the earth,

then I was beside him, like a master worker;[d]
and I was daily his[e] delight,
rejoicing before him always,

rejoicing in his inhabited world
and delighting in the human race.
—PROVERBS 8:22–31

It is the divine page that you must listen to; it is the book of the universe that you must observe. The pages of Scripture can only be read by those who

know how to read and write, while everyone, even the illiterate, can read the book of the universe.
—ST. AUGUSTINE OF HIPPO, ENARRATIONES IN PSALMOS, 45, 7 (PL 36, 518)

Some people, in order to discover God, read a book. But there is a great book: the very appearance of created things. Look above and below, note, read. God whom you want to discover, did not make the letters with ink; he put in front of your eyes the very things that he made. Can you ask for a louder voice than that?
—ST. AUGUSTINE OF HIPPO, C SERMONES, 68, 6

Am I not here, I, who am your Mother? Are you not under my shadow and protection? Am I not the source of your joy? Are you not in the hollow of my mantle, in the crossing of my arms? Do you need anything more? Let nothing else worry you, disturb you."
—OUR LADY OF GUADALUPE TO ST. JUAN DIEGO ON MOUNT TEPAYAC, 1531

On the site of an ancient shrine to the Aztec mother goddess, near Mexico City on Tepeyac Hill, a young Christian Indian named Juan Diego had a vision of a young Indian woman. Speaking in his native tongue, she directed him to tell the bishop to construct a church on the hill. The bishop dismissed the story, but the young maiden appeared yet again to Diego identifying herself as the Mother of God. She instructed him to gather roses that grew at her feet, during the winter no less, and take them to the bishop. When Diego opened his coat, a colorful impression of Our Lady, with dark skin, was imprinted on the fabric.

This story has been told for five hundred years, standing as an "image of divine compassion for a demoralized people. Speaking to Juan Diego in his own language, she presented herself in terms of compassion and solidarity, not power and domination." (Blessed Among Us, December 12, 2020) The image of Our Lady attracts millions of pilgrims each year at the basilica in Mexico City, one of the world's most visited sacred sights.
—FROM: "SACRED MOTHER: OUR LADY OF GUADALUPE." BEINGBENEDICTINE.COM/2020/12/12/SACRED-MOTHER-OUR-LADY-OF-GUADALUPE/

Shakti is called by various names: Pradhana, Prakriti, Maya, Gunavati, Para. She is the mother of cosmic intelligence, without modification. That Shakti is matter-energy (prakriti), the goddess of all and the prime cause and mother of the three gunas.
—SHIVA PURANA, RUDRASAMHITA 1.16

By converging to unity, all things may be accomplished. By the virtue, which is without self-interest, even the supernatural may be subdued.
—CHUANG TZU 12

What I (Earth) speak, I speak with sweetness; What I look at endears itself to me...

Earth, my Mother! Set me securely with bliss in full accord with Heaven. Wise One, uphold me in grace and splendor.
—ATHARVA VEDA 12.1

In the time of the Seventh Fire, a New People would emerge. They would retrace their steps to find the wisdom that was left by the side of the trail long ago. Their steps would take them to the elders, who they would ask to guide them on their journey. If the New People remain strong in their quest, the sacred drum will again sound its voice. There will be an awakening of the people, and the sacred fire will again be lit. At this time, the light-skinned race will be given a choice between two roads. One road is the road of greed and technology without wisdom or respect for life. This road represents a rush to destruction. The other road is spirituality, a slower path that includes respect for all living things. If we choose the spiritual path, we can light yet another fire, an Eight Fire, and begin an extended period of Peace and healthy growth.
—GRANDFATHER WILLIAM COMMANDA, CHIEF OF THE INDIANS OF THE AMERICAS, FOUNDER, CIRCLE OF ALL NATIONS PROPHECY OF THE SEVEN FIRES OF THE ANISHNABE, FROM ANCIENT WAMPUM BELT

All things came into being through him, and without him not one thing came into being.
—JOHN 1:1–5

Acknowledgements

I am full of gratitude for countless people, communities, and organizations who have supported me, my journey, and this book over the years. This is a partial list, knowing it would be impossible to name everyone. I come from a family who makes the world a better place through their passion, their vocations, and their every being. Thank you to my husband, my partner in life, Bryson, for your unending support and love. Thank you for standing beside me with honor and integrity. Our children, Moses, Isaac, and Maria, Bella, keep me full of hope and grateful for our beautiful family. I'm so fortunate to be your mama. For my parents, Evelyn, Bob, and Mary Ann, who surrounded us with love, faith, encouragement and taught us to love serving our community. For my siblings, Paul and Claire and for their spouses, for their beautiful hearts and for the countless memories we share. I have the best in-laws, Brent and Brenda, who model integrity and a love of Christ. For all my sisters-in-laws and brothers-in-laws and every precious cousin. I'm grateful for our beautiful family and each person in it. For my extended family: for Rick who helped me with Justo's story, for Rosy, Shell, Nikki and family. For David and Edwina Haddad, Bob, and TZiPi, who have long supported my spiritual journey and faith.

I also want to acknowledge my ancestors: my grandparents Belia, Raoul, Betty, and Bob, whose faith I seek to honor. For my godparents, Salim and Phyllis Haddad, and Nancy, who taught me so much about

Acknowledgements

Spirit. For Justo and Mercedes Morales, whose strong faith inspires me to this day. For those whose life inspired me but are no longer here: Gary Dimmick, Glenn Busch, and Rhoda Montgomery.

For years, writing this book was a solitary act. Thanks to the NC Writer's Network, Ed Southern, and local writers that encouraged me to share my story. Thank you to friend and poet John Roedel, who has been a constant encourager. Special thanks to my editor, Julia Roller, whose keen eye and understanding my vision for this book has strengthened it. Special thanks to Molly Murphy and Kassie Andreadis for their gifts of editing and design, who turned a manuscript into a book. Special thanks to the team at Pellien PR: Jessica Pellien, Kailey Tse-Harlow, and Trish Banfitch, for sharing the story of this book and the efforts of reform for the church. I'm grateful for photographers Sally McClive and Betsy Blake. For Lauren Harr at Gold Leaf Literary and Jamie Rogers Southern at Bookmarks for their advice and support. For Meghan Ritchie, for your steady support. For Dan Antonelli, friend and encourager. For Karen Jackson, friend and poet. For Rachelle and Cindy DiTiberio.

I'm grateful for Gayle Fisher-Stewart, Erin Weber-Johnson, Mike Kinman, Katie Nakamura-Rengers, Thais Carter, and Elle Dowd, friends and colleagues who believed and worked toward a vision that church reform is possible. Thanks to Tom Brackett, Lydia Bucklin, Amy Huacani, and Matt Visser for their abiding friendship and collegiality. For countless colleagues, parishioners, and friends, lay and ordained, who give me hope for the Episcopal Church. I would like to acknowledge, with thanks, the church leaders who will rise in solidarity for reform. I hold hope in the future of church and it is with faith that I say "thank you" now. For all the church planters, mission redevelopers, and community leaders I have coached that instill hope in me for what is and what could be. A deep bow of thanks to the first circle of women harmed in the church that I worked with. Thank you to all the women over the years who have trusted me with their stories. For C.E.D.A.R., for Dr. Claudia Shields, Mikael Taylor, and their board, for supporting the vision of Water + Light to bring new life to the church through reform and storytelling.

For the many churches, friendship circles, and faith communities I have been a part of. Especially St. Mary's Episcopal, my home church, and the Core Team who helped me plant Christ's Beloved Community Church. So much of what I learned, I learned alongside you. For all the area churches and organizations who partnered with us and supported us, including the Diocese of NC, the NC Synod, Faith Health, and Love Out Loud. For the team at Una Bendición. For our Oasis Circle group. For Ali Tomberlin, who is primarily a steadfast friend, but also an adept attorney who supports me at every turn. For Caroline Brown, whose love for justice is inspiring, and for Chris and Chad, thank you for your enduring friendship. For Christine, Kate, and Michelle, who have each offered wisdom and support. For Linda's gift of healing. For Brenda—for your wise spirit and enduring friendship. For Troy—constant encourager. For Myia—through thick and thin. For the community at the YMCAs I have been a part of and for Camp Pioneer. For the hospitality and community at Prabhupada Village and New Galoka. For the many retreat and conference centers that have nurtured my ability to listen and write, rest, teach, and lead. Special thanks to Connie Hoffner and the staff at Well of Mercy for your sweet hospitality and for your sacred land. For Kanuga, Wild Goose, Lake Logan, and Holden Village. For our beautiful Mother Earth, for all of my schools and places of learning, and for all who have gone before me who have written, sang, and protested for another way.

Above all, I wish to acknowledge Father-Mother God, Jesus Christ, the Virgen de Guadalupe, angels and spirit guides, and my ancestors who inspire and guide me. If any of my words unintentionally cause harm or have characterized God to be anything other than Love, then the mistake is mine. May this book and any ripple effects bring honor to God in all ways, being rooted in Love.

Endnotes

1. The name of the Virgin Mary who appeared to Juan Diego in 1531 in Mexico and is beloved to Mexicans and Mexican-Americans.
2. The canon to the ordinary was the bishop's close assistant and also a priest.
3. A canonical trial is the church version of a legal trial that determines if the defendant is guilty.
4. Mi hija, or mi'ja, means "my daughter."
5. I use the term reign of Love when others might use the term Kingdom of God. It is less colonialistic, and anyone can participate in the reign of Love, rather than exclusively Christians.
6. Dirk Rinker and Michael Jaffarian. "15 Million Americans Have Left Christianity in the Past Ten Years." *ACS Technologies*. July 27, 2022. https://www.acstechnologies.com/church-growth/15-million-americans-have-left-christianity-in-the-past-ten-years/
7. https://www.ncronline.org/news/more-5-billion-spent-catholic-sexual-abuse-allegations-new-report-finds
8. https://www.ncronline.org/news/more-5-billion-spent-catholic-sexual-abuse-allegations-new-report-finds
9. https://www.npr.org/2022/06/02/1102621352/how-the-southern-baptist-convention-covered-up-its-widespread-sexual-abuse-scand
10. In the office of one of the psychologists I met with while recovering from trauma due to harm by my superior, a staff member gave

me an article about the abuse of nuns. The article described the ongoing pattern of sexual abuse of nuns, leading me to wonder if these babies were the product of rape and then intentionally killed to hide the pregnancies. Only God knows.

11 Dr. Clarissa Pinkola Estes, *Women Who Run with The Wolves: Myths and Stories of the Wild Woman Archetype* (New York: Ballantine Books, 1992), 56.
12 Ibid., p.58,
13 DailyMail.com. Special report by Martin Sixsmith. June 7, 2014. https://www.dailymail.co.uk/news/article-2651484/I-thought-Id-seen-Philomena-And-I-nuns-secret-grave-800-babies-By-Martin-Sixsmith-exposed-Sisters-sold-children-fallen-girls.html
14 Ibid.
15 Turner, Frederick. *Beyond Geography: The Western Spirit Against the Wilderness*. Rutgers University Press. New edition 1992.
16 https://skanda987.files.wordpress.com/2016/12/victims-of-the-christian-faith.pdf
17 Little, Becky, "How Early Churches Used Witch Hunts to Gain More Followers", www.history.com. September 1, 2018, https://www.history.com/news/how-churches-used-witch-hunts-to-gain-more-followers and https://www.peterleeson.com/Witch_Trials.pdf
18 Little, Becky, "How Early Churches Used Witch Hunts to Gain More Followers", www.history.com. September 1, 2018, https://www.history.com/news/how-churches-used-witch-hunts-to-gain-more-followers
19 Equal Justice Initiative, "The Transatlantic Slave Trade" (2022).
20 Fisher-Stewart, Gayle. *Church Hurt: Reparations for My Soul: Healing Racialized Trauma*. 2024. Opening page.
21 Onishi, Bradley. Uncovering the (White) Christian Roots of Slavery, Native American Genocide, And Ongoing Efforts to Erase History. https://religiondispatches.org/uncovering-the-white-christian-roots-of-slavery-native-american-genocide-and-ongoing-efforts-to-erase-history/

Endnotes

22 US Indian Boarding School History, National Native American Boarding School Healing Coalition website: https://boardingschoolhealing.org/education/us-indian-boarding-school-history/
23 Isaiah 43:19 "I am about to do a new thing; now it springs forth, do you not perceive it? I will make a way in the wilderness and rivers in the desert."
24 Marriage was not allowed for LGBTQ people in the United States at this time. Yet I was fortunate to serve an Episcopal Church that welcomed and affirmed LGBTQ people long before our country sanctioned their love.
25 By church, I mean the collective body of followers of Jesus Christ, any time where two or three (or more) are gathered. I do not limit the definition of church to institutional church, denominations, or churches with buildings or paid clergy.
26 Note that Christ consciousness, God's Rhema, and the Divine Feminine are covered in chapters 5, 6, and 7.
27 Proverbs 8:30
28 Proverbs 8:22, 27, 30 "The Lord created me at the beginning of his work, the first of his acts long ago. When he established the heavens, I was there, when he drew a circle on the face of the deep, then I was beside him, like a master worker; and I was daily his delight."
29 John 1:3
30 John 18:36
31 More about how to do this and other techniques referenced in this book will be explained in my second book.
32 The Divine Mother, the counterpart to God the Father, has been unacknowledged by Christianity for centuries. I choose to capitalize her pronouns out of deep respect, and as a counterbalance to most of history, when She has been cast aside.
33 Refer to Vine Deloria Jr.'s books for further reading on this subject.

34 Learn more at rootthrivesoar.com.
35 I often mention Mary, the Mother of God, since my focus is on the other side of God the Father. There are certainly other women who embody the Sacred Feminine, such as Mary Magdalene, who are worthy of reclaiming as we seek a fuller expression of the Divine.
36 Such as Parmahansa Yogananda and Eckhart Tolle.
37 Learn more at contemporarymysticspublishing.com.
38 Mark 9:24
39 "So God created humankind[a] in his image, in the image of God he created them; male and female he created them." Genesis 1:27, NRSV
40 Matthew 9:22, Mark 5:34, Mark 10:52, Luke 8:48, Luke 18:42
41 This process is renewing for followers of Jesus. See rootthrivesoar.com for quotes from missional practitioners. One said, "God is in our neighbors. To serve God means to meet God in our neighbors and we cannot do that without stepping out [of the church building]."
42 Richard Rohr uses this term to describe church as it has been, compared to what it could be.
43 2 Corinthians 4:7
44 "Abide in me as I abide in you."—John 15:4
45 Quotes are from multiple sources, including *World Scripture: A Comparative Anthology of Sacred Texts*, 1995.

About the Author

Chantal McKinney is a mystic Christian and visionary, a faith-based entrepreneur, nationwide speaker, coach, and consultant for a wide diversity of churches, faith communities, and non-profits. She spent several years following Jesus beyond church walls by cultivating relationships and holy loitering in Section 8 housing, on sidewalks, and in the tiendas of Southside Winston-Salem when she was healing from church trauma. Her deep community work led to her becoming the founding pastor for Christ's Beloved Community/Comunidad Amada de Cristo. She later founded Root Thrive Soar, a parachurch organization that trains, equips, and empowers churches, faith communities, and circles around the country to engage in compassionate action and mutual ministry within their local communities in the spirit of Christ's love. Originally ordained as a priest in the Episcopal Church at the age of twenty-five, she now continually strives to be God's priest, with a particular heart for the millions of people who are in exile and on the margins of church. She is honored to form circles for those that cannot find a home in church, including those who are spiritually expansive and women who have been harmed in church. She founded

Water + Light with colleagues and friends to midwife new life in the church, to shine a light on the shadow side of church, and to cultivate healing, justice, and reform. When her experience and spiritual wisdom did not fit neatly within the traditional publishing world, she founded Contemporary Mystics Publishing. She seeks to support other authors who want to publish books rooted in Divine Love that expand our faith and spirituality beyond the confines of a patriarchal concept of God. She lives in North Carolina with her husband and their three children.

Learn more at:
chantalmckinney.com
rootthrivesoar.com
contemporarymysticspublishing.com

If you have experienced harm in the church, visit the author's website to learn how you can share your story through Water + Light.

www.ingramcontent.com/pod-product-compliance
Lightning Source LLC
LaVergne TN
LVHW040043080526
838202LV00045B/3473